Sacred Christmas Music

The Stories Behind the Most Beloved Songs of Devotion

Ronald M. Clancy

STERLING

New York / London
www.sterlingpublishing.com/kids

Translators

Hodie Christus natus est—Ronald M. Clancy (b. 1944)
Hört zu ihr lieben Leute—Ezra Harold Geer (1886–1957)
Jesu, bleibet mein freude—Robert S. Bridges (1844–1930)
Panis angelicus—Gerald Malsbary (b. 1950)
Stille nacht, heiligen nacht—John Freeman Young (1820–85)
Veni, Emmanuel—Thomas Alexander Lacey (1853–1931)

Hört zu ihr lieben Leute: English translation by Ezra Harold Geer
courtesy of Moseler Verlag, Wolfenbüttel, Germany. © All rights reserved.

Library of Congress Cataloging-in-Publication Data Available

10 9 8 7 6 5 4 3 2 1

Published by Sterling Publishing Co., Inc.
387 Park Avenue South, New York, NY 10016
© 2008 by Ronald M. Clancy
Distributed in Canada by Sterling Publishing
c/o Canadian Manda Group, 165 Dufferin Street
Toronto, Ontario, Canada M6K 3H6
Distributed in the United Kingdom by GMC Distribution Services
Castle Place, 166 High Street, Lewes, East Sussex, England BN7 1XU
Distributed in Australia by Capricorn Link (Australia) Pty. Ltd.
P.O. Box 704, Windsor, NSW 2756, Australia

Printed in China
All rights reserved

Sterling ISBN 978-1-4027-5811-9

For information about custom editions, special sales, premium and
corporate purchases, please contact Sterling Special Sales
Department at 800-805-5489 or specialsales@sterlingpublishing.com.

Contents

List of Illustrations

Front cover: Gaudenzio Ferrari (c.1475–1546), Italian, *The Concert of Angels,* 1534–36 fresco detail, Sanctuary of Santa Maria delle Grazie, Saronno, Italy / The Bridgeman Art Library

Page 12: *Madonna and Child Enthroned with Two Angels,* 1480 oil on panel Hans Memling (c. 1433–1494), German-Flemish Galleria degli Uffizi, Florence

Page 16: Philippe de Champaigne (1602–1674), French, *The Nativity,* 1643 oil on canvas, Musée des Beaux-Arts, Lille / The Bridgeman Art Library

Page 19: *First Page of "The Gospel According to St. Luke 2:1-12,"* 4th–5th century Greek brown ink on parchment, Washington MS. III (W), Freer Gallery of Art, Smithsonian Institute, Washington, DC

Page 20: Fra Angelico (c.1387–1455), Italian (Florentine), *The Nativity with St. Catherine of Alexandria and St. Peter the Martyr,* 1442 fresco, Museo di San Marco dell' Angelico, Florence / The Bridgeman Art Library

Page 23: *Concert,* first century A.D. wall mural from Stabiae (near Pompeii), Museo Archeologico Nazionale, Naples / Giraudon / The Bridgeman Art Library

Page 24: Herbert Gute (1908–1977), American, *Consecration of the Tabernacle,* 2nd century reconstructed wall painting from synagogue at Dura Europus, Syria, Yale University Art Library

Page 27: *St. Gregory,* c.870 illumination from a Sacramentary fragment of Metz, School of Corbie, MS. Latin 1141, fol. 3r, Bibliothèque Nationale de France, Paris

Page 28: Jean Fouquet (c.1420–1481), French, *Charlemagne Crowned Emperor by Pope Leo III on December 25, 800 A.D. at St. Peter's in Rome,* c.1455 illumination from *Grandes chroniques de France* (Second livre de Charlemagne), MS. Francais 6465, fol. 89v, Bibliothèque Nationale de France, Paris

Page 31: *Guido d'Arezzo with His Pupil Archbishop Theodaldus,* 12th century manuscript illumination from Codex 51, fol. 35v, Oesterreichische Nationalbibliothek, Vienna

Page 33: *A Troubadour,* 14th century illumination on vellum from *Livre des Cent Ballades,* by Jean le Sénéchal (French School), Musée Condé, Chantilly, France/ The Bridgeman Art Library

Page 34: Jean Fouquet (c.1420–1481), French, *Etienne Chevalier and His Patron Paying Homage to the Virgin and Child,* manuscript illumination, MS. Francais 71, fol.1, Musée Condé, Chantilly, France / Lauros / Giraudon / The Bridgeman Art Library

Page 36: *A Carole in the Orchard,* from *Le Roman de la Rose,* c.1460 illuminated manuscript, MS. Francais 19153, fol. 7, Bibliothèque Nationale de France, Paris

Page 38: *The Organ as Symbol of the Church,* early 15th century English miniature from *Thomas a Kempis, Liber interne consolacionis,* MS. Royal 7B.VIII, fol. 3, British Library, London

Page 39: Hans Memling (c.1433–1494), Netherlandish, *Angels Playing Musical Instruments,* c.1487-90 oil on right panel of triptych from Church of Santa Maria la Real, Najera, Spain, Koninklijk Museum voor Schone Kunsten, Antwerp, Belgium / The Bridgeman Art Library

Page 41: Rossello Franchi (1377–1456) and Filippo Torelli (1409–1468), Italian, *Historiated initial 'P' depicting the Nativity,* Corale/Graduale no.5 manuscript illumination, Museo dell'Opera del Duomo, Prato, Italy / The Bridgeman Art Library

Page 45: Emanuel De Witte (c.1616–1692), Dutch, *A Gothic Protestant Church,* 1685 oil on canvas, The State Hermitage Museum, St. Petersburg

Page 46: *Johann Sebastian Bach Playing and Conducting in Concert in 1714 in the Chapel Choir of Weimar,* engraving after a painting by H.W. Schmidt (active late 18th century), German, Lebrecht Music & Arts Photo Library, London

Page 47: Francois Marius Granet (1775–1849), French, *Interior of the Choir in the Capuchin Church on the Piazza Barberini in Rome,* c.1820 oil on canvas, The State Hermitage Museum, St. Petersburg

Page 49: Luigi Mussini (1813–1888), Italian (Florentine), *Sacred Music,* 1841 oil on canvas, Galleria dell' Accademia, Florence/ The Bridgeman Art Library

Page 53: Jan Van Eyck (c.1390–1441) and Hubert Van Eyck (c.1370-1426), Netherlandish, *Singing Angels,* 1432 oil on left panel from Ghent altarpiece *Adoration of the Lamb,* St. Bavo Cathedral, Ghent, Belgium / The Bridgeman Art Library

Page 54: Edward Timothy Hurley (1869–1950), American, *The Midnight Mass,* 1911 oil on canvas, Cincinnati Art Museum, Gift of Mr. and Mrs. Simon Hubig, Accession #1911.1372

Page 56: Edward Burne-Jones (1833–1898), English designer, *Alleluia,* c.1885 tapestry, Harris Museum and Art Gallery, Lancashire, UK / The Bridgeman Art Library

Page 59: Pieter Bruegel, the Elder (1525–1569), Flemish, *The Massacre of the Innocents,* c.1565 oil on panel, Kunsthistorisches Museum, Vienna

Page 60: *Title Page of Concerto Grossi Op. 6,* 1690 Arcangelo Corelli music score published posthumously c.1714, manuscript M1040.C79, Op.6, Music Division, Library of Congress, Washington, DC © Photograph by Ronald M. Clancy

Page 61: Giorgione (c.1478–1510), Italian (Venetian), *The Adoration of the Shepherds,* c.1505-10 oil on canvas, National Gallery of Art, Washington, DC / The Bridgeman Art Library

Page 62: *Josquin Desprez,* 1611 woodcut after a cathedral painting by Petrus Opmeer (1526–1595), Dutch, for *Opus chronographicum orbis universi a mundi,* Lebrecht Music & Art Collection, London

Page 63: *The Nativity,* 1490 illumination from *The Sforza Hours,* manuscript BL, Additional MS. 34294, fol. 82v. - with Flemish additions in 1519, British Library, London

Page 64: *St. Gregory's Holy Words Written on a Tablet by Monk,* c.983 illumination from "Registrum Gregorii," 1MS. 1171/626, Stadbibliothek, Trier, Germany

Page 65: *Genealogy of Christ According to "Gospel of St. Matthew" in French Neumes,* 9th century *Gospel of Corbie* notated illuminated manuscript, MS. Latin 11958, fol. 14, Bibliothèque Nationale de France, Paris

Page 68: *Gradual from a Christmas Mass,* mid-12th century manuscript page from St. Alban's Abbey, MS. 2.B. 1V, fol. 24v, British Library, London

Page 69: Limbourg Brothers (active c.1400–1416), Flemish, *The Celebration of Christmas Mass at Sainte Chapelle, Paris,* illumination from *Les Très Riches Heures du Duc du Berry,* MS. 65/1284, fol. 158r, Musée Condé, Chantilly, France / The Bridgeman Art Library

Page 70: Follower of Fra Angelico (c.1387–1455), Italian (Florentine), *The Virgin and Child with Angels,* c.1445 tempera on panel, National Gallery of Art, London / The Bridgeman Art Library

Page 71: *Prosperous Couple on Way to Church,* Flemish, late 15th century manuscript illustration, Clm. 28345, fol. 2r, Bayerische Staatabibliothek, Munich

Page 73: Raphael (Raffaello Sanzio of Urbino)(1483–1520), Italian, *The Sistine Madonna,* 1513 oil on canvas, Staatliche Kunstsammlungen: Gemaldegalerie Alte Meister, Dresden / The Bridgeman Art Library

Page 74: Martin Schongauer (c.1445–1491), German, *The Annunciation,* c.1470 tempera on wood panel from the *Orlier Altarpiece,* Musée d'Unterlinden, Colmar, France/ The Bridgeman Art Library

Page 76: *The Visitation,* 15th century, German School Musee de l'Oeuvre de Notre Dame, Strasbourg, France

Page 79: *St. Thomas Church and School, Leipzig,* Johann Gottfried Krügner the Elder, German, 1723 engraving, Bach-Archiv, Leipzig / The Bridgeman Art Library

Page 80: *Title page of "Missarum liber primus,"* 1554 Mass music book, MS. 1572, fol. K.9.a.6, British Library, London / Lebrecht Music & Arts Photo Library

Page 81: Antonio Allegri Correggio (1489–1534), Italian, *The Nativity (La Notte),* c.1525 oil on burlap, Staatliche Kunstsammlungen: Gemaldegalerie Alte Meister, Dresden / The Bridgeman Art Library

Page 82: Albrecht Durer (1471–1528), German, *Hands of an Apostle,* 1508 brush drawing, Graphische Sammlung Albertina, Vienna, Austria / The Bridgeman Art Library

Page 83: Paolo Veronese (1528–1588), Italian, *The Eternal Father,* c.1555 oil on canvas, Hospital Tavera, Toledo, Spain / The Bridgeman Art Library

Page 84: F. W. Fairhold (1814–1866), *Neal's Music Hall,* Fishamble Street, Dublin, c.1850 drawing, Lebrecht Music & Arts Photo Collection, London

Page 85: Thomas Hudson (1701–1779), British, *George Frederic Handel,* 1756 oil on canvas, National Portrait Gallery, London / Lebrecht Music & Arts Photo Collection, London

Page 87: *Title Page from "Messiah Oratorio,"* 1767 music score with alterations made earlier by George Frederic Handel (1685–1759), manuscript M2000.H22 M26, Music Division, Library of Congress, Washington, DC © Photograph by Ronald M. Clancy

Page 88: El Greco (1541–1614), Spanish, *The Nativity,* c.1605 oil on canvas, Church of Charity, Illescas, Toledo, Spain / Lauros / Giraudon / The Bridgeman Art Library

Page 91: *St. Thomas Aquinas at Prayer,* c.1492 illumination from the *Psalter and Hours of Alphonso V of Aragon,* MS. Add 28962, fol. 36, British Library, London

Page 92: Fritz von Uhde (1848–1911), German, *Holy Night,* oil on panel triptych, Staatliche Kunstsammlungen: Gemaldegalerie Neue Meister, Dresden

Page 95: Karl Friedrich Lessing (1808–1880), German, *Cloister in the Snow,* 1829 oil on canvas, Wallraff-Richartz-Museum, Cologne, Germany

Page 97: *Nuns with Prayer Books at Church Services,* c.1300 illumination from *La Sainte Abbaye,* MS. YT11, fol. 6v, British Library, London

Page 101: *Choir of Monks and Their Leader,* late 14th century French miniature from *La Bible hystoriaux,* MS. Francais 159, fol. 277v, Bibliothèque Nationale France, Paris

Acknowledgments

TO FRIENDS AND FAMILY ALIKE whose strong support over the years has enabled me to persevere and overcome all adversity and the doubts of publishing and music industry insiders who considered my series of Christmas music collections as an overly ambitious enterprise.

Special thanks go to Sterling Publishing, the only publisher willing to support the unique concept of fusing an illustrated history of Christmas music, whose pages are adorned by magnificent art, and beautiful music CDs in a seamless package.

A great debt is also owed to the following people and organizations: staff members of the Library of Congress Music Division; the Philadelphia Free Library Music Department staff, especially Linda Wood, who was ever faithful in her support; the staff of the Van Pelt Library of the University of Pennsylvania; Prof. William Studwell, a rich resource and authority on Christmas carols; Doug Anderson, a wonderful Internet carol resource and author of www.TheHymnsandCarolsofChristmas.com; Nancy Taube of Highland Music Engraving; Sister Gerald Vincent McDevitt, SSJ, and Sister Anna Josephine Bennis, SSJ, Philadelphia, Pennsylvania; Todd Wilmot and Prof. Gerald Malsbary of St. Charles Borromeo Seminary in Philadelphia; and the late Adrianne Onderdonk Dudden, a remarkable woman, dear friend, terrific book designer, and faithful collaborator.

For their incisive comments and special attention to detail, gifted musicologists provided welcome clarifications pertaining to *The Historical Perspective,* especially Dr. Richard R. Bunbury, assistant professor of music at Boston University, who provided immeasurable expert consultation and patience throughout the process of reviewing and re-reviewing several texts, as well as Prof. Scott Fogelsong, chair of music theory and musicianship at the San Francisco Conservatory, and Prof. John Poole of the Choral Conducting Department at Indiana University.

For helping with the difficult task of assembling the representative images, I am ever grateful to a host of dedicated art librarians, including staff personnel from the Pennsylvania Academy of Fine Arts, Philadelphia; the University of Pennsylvania Fine Arts Library; the Moore School of Art & Design; Deborah Litwack and her Art Department staff of the Free Library of Philadelphia; various art photo agencies, especially Ed Whitley of the Bridgeman International Art Library; and curators and rights personnel from some of the world's prominent museums and libraries.

Others deserving special mention are current and former staff personnel of SONY-BMG Music Special Products, for their unceasing support of the concept of fusing music, art, and history in special packages.

All of these individuals and organizations confirmed the value of cooperation, thus making *Sacred Christmas Music* a true team effort.

R.M.C.

Sacred Christmas Music

Preface

CHRISTMAS IS CELEBRATED by tens of millions of people around the world. Its universal themes of peace to all humankind, generosity, and joy in salvation are central to Christians in every land and time. For us today, it is a season imbued with warm and loving sights and sounds that stir up memories of cherished times with family and friends. Christmas music is often the common uniting force in social gatherings—people listen to and join in the singing of the music of the season. Christmas music transcends religious inclinations, even in this secular and commercial age. Through the maze of shopping and parties, the simple joys of the holiday reach our hearts most powerfully through the music.

Carols, Christmas trees, gifts, and other elements we associate with Christmas, began gaining their present popularity in the nineteenth century, many having been brought to America from German-speaking lands. In earlier times, Christmas had a more distinctly devotional focus. It followed the somberly penitential season of Advent, with days of spiritual rejoicing and communal feasting. This contrast, as Lent is to Easter, made the celebratory nature of the birth of Christ a palpable reality. Christmas extended its influence to all cultures and levels of society, from within the cathedral and village church to the home and village market. Most important, the almost universally significant influence of Christmas made a lasting impression on the culture, art, and spirituality of our European ancestors.

Our need to experience the wealth of the arts and tradition related to the Nativity, and to understand its importance in human history, is as great as it ever has been in these last two millennia; hence, the need for *Sacred Christmas Music.* This volume takes the reader through a journey in time from the dawn of Christian music in the Church's liturgical song through the great choral and instrumental works of the Baroque era to representative pieces of the twentieth century. The sacred tradition of music is explored through vocal and instrumental music of a variety of national and historical periods and styles, whose importance has earned them a place in the canon of great musical masterpieces. Not only will you have a guide that is easily accessible for the musician and non-musician alike, but you will feast in a sumptuous gallery of thematically and historically corresponding full-color art, reveling in what are arguably among the best performances and recordings of the music ever made. Rest assured that there is no other collection that will bring together all these elements in such an aesthetically pleasing and educational way.

In my work as a liturgical and concert organist, choral and orchestral conductor, and professor of music history of many years, I have tried to communicate through performance, liturgy, and teaching the richness of meaning inherent in the celebration of Christmas and its great music throughout Western civilization. Mr. Ronald Clancy, the author of *Sacred Christmas Music,* has achieved what I could only dream of. The quality, breadth, and depth of this collection constitute a truly astonishing achievement and a valuable gift for families to treasure for many years to come.

Richard R. Bunbury, PhD
Boston University

Madonna and Child Enthroned with Two Angels
1480 oil on panel
Hans Memling (c. 1433–1494),
German-Flemish
Galleria degli Uffizi, Florence

Introduction

THE SEED OF INSPIRATION for *Sacred Christmas Music* was sown many years ago on a Christmas Eve when I was one of hundreds of boys at St. John's Orphanage in Philadelphia. To this day I have never forgotten the warm flush and feeling of wonderment, despite the drowsiness of the late hour, when first entering the fir-scented orphanage chapel and taking in my first Midnight Mass. The carols and sacred music I heard on that memorable occasion kindled a love for Christmas music that has remained with me throughout the years.

It would be many more years before I heard more special music for Christmas. Although less popularly known, these motets, oratorios, Italian Baroque Christmas concertos, and other forms of ancient Christmas music affected me in a genuine and positive way. When I heard these sacred pieces at various Advent and Christmas church services during the early 1980s, I was moved to learn more about the entire spectrum of Christmas music. And it was at this point where my fascination with Christmas music became a fixation and a desire to share my enthusiasm for the subject.

Over the following years I accumulated an extensive library of Christmas music. During the course of this period I often thought about the origins and development of Christmas music. There were always intriguing questions: When did music celebrating the birth of Christ begin? What did it sound like in the early centuries of Christianity, the Middle Ages, and the Renaissance? Many books have been published about Christmas music, predominant among them carol collections, but there has hardly been any definitive work specifically tracing the evolution of Christmas music from the early years of Christianity to the modern era.

Also, I felt that the whole body of Christmas music is considerably more than the few traditional religious and secular standards that are repeatedly played each Christmas season. Some of the very best Christmas music is performed at various churches or concert halls during Advent and Christmastide as part of musical programs staged by professional or amateur groups. These fine works are unfamiliar to many people.

When my friends suggested I pursue the idea of writing about the topic, I took their suggestion with a little trepidation because their concept of the project was considerably different from the ambitious vision I had. They thought I should write a book on the topic. My idea was to create a series of richly illustrated books with magnificent art packaged with beautiful music CDs. I began the project in earnest in 1989, and, as is the case in most labors of love, there were many moments of frustration, as I tried to locate specific historical information. Eventually, my first book on the subject of Christmas music, *Best Loved Christmas Carols,* was born, followed by *American Christmas Classics* and *Children's Christmas Classics. Sacred Christmas Music* is my fourth volume on this topic and the one closest to my heart.

To some degree *Sacred Christmas Music* is similar in its objectives to my initial offerings. What distinguishes it from the others, however, is a hopeful premise that it can be considered as a worthy primer on the history of Western music, even though it comes through the prism of music devoted to Christmas.

In my effort to enhance the enjoyment and learning experience about the history of Christmas music, I tried to accomplish the following goals:

• to compile a desirable collection of Christmas music, including a few carols, strictly dedicated to sacred themes;

• to include rich, interesting background information about each musical work;

• to provide a concise and informative historical perspective about the origins and development of Christmas music on a dual track with the history of Western music, thus allowing the reader to understand the cultural context of Christmas music and how this sacred music might have sounded at given moments in time, from the earliest days of Christianity to the twentieth century;

• to adorn the book with beautiful illustrations and art relating to Christmas music, or the Christmas story and tradition, many of them paintings from the great museums of the Western world or colorful manuscript illuminations from such pre-eminent institutions as the British Library in London and the Bibliothèque Nationale de France in Paris;

• to supplement the illustrated history of Christmas music and text with an exquisite audio collection incorporating hymns and carols, but mostly Gregorian chant and distinguished polyphonic or instrumental works specifically composed for the ancient Christmas Mass and the canonical hours of Advent or Christmas, and the theme of the Nativity.

Sacred Christmas Music is the legacy I hope to leave to devotees of Christmas music. Perhaps families of professional musicians and nonprofessionals alike will share it, and upon hearing this special music, their spirits will soar to celestial heights, and once there, find comfort in the contemplative melodies that quietly arouse and confirm belief in the omnipotence of a Supreme Being.

It is by design that the music chosen for *Sacred Christmas Music* is of a deeply religious character. Think as though entering the Holy of Holies to worship, to seek meaning in one's everyday existence—its daily labor, the joys and disappointments, love and its afflictions, and maybe even the inevitable question of being. Then seek spiritual comfort in contemplating the very beginning of Christian belief, the birth of a wonderful child over two thousand years ago, a birth celebrated today as the Nativity of Our Lord and Savior Jesus Christ.

This singular event has inspired some of the most magnificent art and majestic sounds of the Western world, and it is these two great pillars of the humanities that elevate *Sacred Christmas Music* in an effort to add new luster to the Christmas repertoire.

The Nativity
1643 oil on canvas
Philippe de Champaigne
(1602–1674), French
Musée des Beaux-Arts, Lille

The Historical Perspective

SACRED CHRISTMAS MUSIC is an expansion into the realm of the origins of Christmas music. At the same time it is an effort to briefly explore and explain the development of Western music, a crucial element and without which the history of Christian music cannot effectively be told. What differentiates this volume from previous collections I have compiled is the predominance of classical and instrumental works—including excerpts from Handel's *Messiah*, motets, Latin hymns, and Gregorian chant for Christmas Masses. Before turning to the music program, let us first delve into the evolution of Christmas as a Church feast day and the development of sacred Christmas music, which indeed is a window to understanding Western Music

CHRISTMAS AND WINTER CELEBRATIONS

Winter has been a favorite time for celebrations for the past five thousand years. Before Christ was born in Bethlehem, pagan Europe and Rome reveled during the winter solstice, generally occurring around December 22, when the sun returning to the northern skies was at its weakest. Because the days were gray and cold, and the nights colder and long, reveling was a favorite thing to do from Rome to Scandinavia. This practice of celebrating continues to this very day in the form of merry-making at Christmas.

The winter solstice would give rise to popular Roman festivals of *Dies Natalis Solis Invicti*, the Feast of Lights or the Day of the Invincible Sun, Saturnalia, and Kalends, and in other countries the festivals of Yuletide, Wassail, and the New Year. *Dies Natalis Solis Invicti* was celebrated by the lighting of huge bonfires, by processions, and by prayer. Saturnalia, occurring during the period of December 17 to 23 was the most popular festival, commemorating Saturn, the god of agriculture ruling the world during a legendary Golden Age, a time when men and women wore garlands in their hair as they carried lights in procession. During Kalends, the first three days of January, people decorated evergreens with lights, and the giving of presents, such as green wreaths, to friends and invited guests was commonplace. Kalends was also the time when rich and poor, slaves and masters, all danced, feasted, and participated in games. The exchange of gifts was always an important part of these festivities.

Although not the most significant Roman festival, a distinction enjoyed by Saturnalia, *Dies Natalis Solis Invicti* was celebrated in honor of Mithras, the Persian god of light and sacred contracts who was born out of a rock on December 25. Early Church officials assigned the birth of Christ to *Dies Natalis Solis Invicti* on December 25 on the Julian calendar because they wanted a Christian feast to substitute for the pagan festivals. In addition, they wanted to offset the cult of the sun, which was particularly strong in the fourth century. Their efforts were certainly aided by the conversion of the Emperor Constantine (288–337 A.D.) to Christianity in 312 A.D. and his Edict of Toleration issued the following year. With the emergence of the Church from persecution status to a religion encouraged by the state under Constantine, and with the Council of Nicaea (325 A.D.) acting to bring unity to it and its complex liturgy, the Church was able to counter pagan practices and to intrude in many areas of secular life.

The celebration of Christmas in the first three centuries was quite different and certainly less elaborate than it is now. It was considered the commemoration of a historical event, rather than a mystery feast of the Church, and it coincided with pagan festivities of the winter solstice. *Jul,* better known as *Yule,* a Scandinavian festival that lasted for twelve days from late December to early January, was a time when people celebrated their faith in the arrival of spring and warmth by decorating fir trees, which didn't lose their leaves in winter. It was a time, too, when people gave each other wheat, since food was scarce. December also was the darkest month, and in Scandinavia the days were even shorter than those experienced by the Romans. Scandinavians celebrated by burning Yule logs to bring good luck and warmth to their homes to combat both the cold and darkness in hope of reviving the fading sun. In Britain, Druids celebrated the victory of evergreens over winter's darkness. In later centuries, Wassail would be celebrated by the English by drinking fermented spirits from the wassail bowl. Crafted from pewter or silver, the bowl could be enormous in size, and people from the poorer classes would drink tangy spiced mead or mulled wine from it in return for their singing and dancing. In central Europe the pagans believed that with the death of the old sun, witches and demons would descend on earth to destroy the fertility of the New Year, and gift giving was prescribed as preventive medicine against such dark happenings.

Some aspects of Winter Solstice celebrations would evolve as part of Christmas tradition, including the decorating of evergreens, a custom quickly adopted by the barbarians who returned to Germany from Rome during the fourth to sixth centuries, eating and drinking beyond moderation, burning Yule logs, and singing and dancing. Christians absorbed these pagan customs of the winter solstice and made them part of Christmas celebrations in their efforts to spread the faith.

St. Gregory the Great in the late sixth century encouraged adopting some pagan customs as another method of spreading Christianity. One way this could be accomplished was by destroying religious idols and altars without doing the same to the buildings so that the pagans could still use the same familiar premises for worshipping Jesus Christ. Eventually in the northern countries of Europe, the feast of the Nativity replaced the peasant rites of the winter solstice, even though the actual date of Christ's birth is uncertain.

No mention of the date appears in the Gospels, although the book of Luke (2:2) comes closest to providing a clue. Luke states that Christ was born in Bethlehem, a town in the kingdom of Judea, at the time of a census undertaken by Cyrinus, the governor of Syria, and during the reign of Caesar Augustus (30 B.C.–14 A.D.). It is known that a census had taken place in Judea sometime during Cyrinus's administration and before Judea was officially incorporated into the province of Syria in 6 A.D. Most scholars are inclined to believe the Nativity occurred in the 8–6 B.C. period.

The celebration of Christmas during the early centuries after Christ's birth, however, was done with great trepidation because of serious religious persecution and martyrdom. The first mention of the Nativity may have come from Pope St. Clement (c.91–100A.D.), the third successor to St. Peter who counseled his

First Page of "The Gospel According to St. Luke 2:1-12"
4th–5th century Greek brown ink on parchment
Freer Gallery of Art,
Smithsonian Institution,
Washington

followers thusly: "Brethren, keep diligently all feast days, and truly in the first place, the day of Christ's birth." In 303 A.D. the Roman Emperor Diocletian commemorated the Nativity by putting twenty thousand Christians to death by fire. Many of the early saints of the Christian Church were martyrs who refused to renounce their faith.

The celebration of Christmas as a church feast day was a reality by the fourth century. Several sources mention it. Christmas was cited in the *Roman Chronograph* of 354 A.D., an ancient almanac and calendar that contained the *Depositio martyrum,* first written in 336 A.D. listing the dates and locations where solemn Christian feasts for martyrs were observed in Rome. One of the oldest Christmas sermons found, given in 383 A.D. by Optatus of Mileve in Numidia, a part of North Africa, notes the feast, and Christmas was known in Milan, Italy, and in Tarragona, Spain. A wall painting that depicts a Nativity scene, or the crèche, decorates the catacombs of San Sebastian, Rome, indicating a Christian family living around 380 A.D. celebrated Christmas.

In 392 A.D. Emperor Theodosius I (c.346–395 A.D.) officially outlawed paganism, paving the way for the commemoration of Christ's birth. By the mid-fifth century, Christmas was on the calendar of Perpetuus, the Bishop of Tours from 461 to 491 A.D. Even in the Eastern Church, by the end of the fourth century, in places such as Constantinople, Antioch, and Alexandria, where the Nativity was celebrated on January 6, the Western Church feast of December 25 was acknowledged as the observed date.

Christmas officially became a major feast day when Pope Leo I, known as Leo the Great (440–461 A.D.), one of the great figures in the development of liturgy and its music, declared it as the liturgical celebration of the Mystery of the Incarnation.

Christmas, a word derived from Old English *Cristes Maesse,* or *Cristes-messe,* literally means the Mass of Christ. The earliest practice of Midnight Mass may have originated at Bethlehem. Pope Sixtus III (432–440 A.D.), who admired the service

there, instituted it as part of Christmas worship. The Mass at dawn may have imitated the sixth-century liturgy of Palestine that commemorated the Byzantine martyr Anastasia. The Third Mass, the oldest and most central liturgy, was celebrated in the more primitive basilica of St. Peter in Rome.

It was also during the sixth century when Dionysius Exiguus ("the Little"), a scholarly Scythian monk who lived in Rome (c.500–545 A.D.) and whose special fields of study were canon law and ecclesiastical chronology, created the Christian calendar after he had investigated Christ's birth date. He determined it had occurred in the year 753 of the Roman calendar, thus starting the practice of dating events as A.D., or *anno domini nostri Jesu Christi,* which means "in the year of our Lord Jesus Christ," and using that date as a separation point for dividing history. Dionysius's calculations for the birth of Christ, nonetheless, were several years off the mark, and scholars have since estimated the Nativity occurred sometime between 8 and 6 B.C. It was not until 1627 when Petavius (1583–1652), born Denis Pétau, a French Jesuit theologian, invented the system of dating events prior to the birth of Christ, or B.C. ("before Christ"). The first name adopted by Petavius, coincidentally, was Dionysius. Our calendar today reflects these dating systems developed by Dionysius Exiguus and Dionysius Petavius.

During the seventh and eighth centuries, the structure of the Christmas season continued to take form within the Church. Advent, meaning "coming," was designated as a time of fasting and penance in preparation of the feast of the Nativity. Its meaning is two-fold. The theology of awaiting the Messiah not only had to do with his incarnation, but it also encompassed the nation of Christ's Second Coming at the end of time. In addition, Advent was designated the official beginning of the church year.

In the eighth century, the Christmas season encompassed the period of Advent, four Sundays before Christmas Day, and ended with Candlemas, a February 2 feast day honoring the Presentation of the Infant Child in the Temple and the Purification of the Virgin Mary. Candlemas was celebrated by lighted candles, hence its name.

By the ninth century, Christmas was firmly established on the church calendar, and great developments were occurring in the world of music.

The Early Years of Western Music

Western music was in some ways simpler in the early days of Christianity. In the age of Roman rule, music was primarily composed for poetry. In fact, the term "music" designated "sung poetry" in ancient times. Choral music was popular, but it was generally sung in one voice no matter what the vocal ranges of the singers. Singing in two, three, or four voices was probably not in practice. The basic musical instruments of the time were the aulos—an ancient Greek and prominent reed instrument, more similar to the oboe than the flute—and the lyre. The aulos accompanied drama, while the lyre, a harp-like instrument with a history dating as far back as 3000 B.C., was normally used for songs. In brief, there was little innovation to Western music in the early stages of the first millennium.

The advance of Western music was given its greatest shove to glory by the Christian Church. It is imperative, if one wants to fully appreciate the general history of Western music, to be able to link it directly with the liturgy. There is very little history of folk or non-liturgical music in the Western world until the late Middle Ages, save for precious few extant examples of notated secular music. Although there are many documents that provide evidence for the practice of (or against) music, which of itself constitutes a rich history, one might see how music was made to become a servant of the Christian faith by making the connection to church liturgy.

The liturgical organization of the Mass for the early Christian Church was partly based on the Jewish set of services. This was understandable since the Apostles and the first Christian disciples were Jews who accepted Jesus Christ as the promised Messiah. It is this heritage that allowed for the Jewish form of biblical worship to take hold as the basic structure of Christian worship within sixty years of Christ's death and resurrection. The extensive use of the Bible for worship was an integral part of the liturgical rite of the Jerusalem Church, begun by St. James, its first bishop, which set the standards of worship for the new churches from Antioch to Rome. It was not until the fourth century that liturgical books made their appearance.

Early church music was a form of chant derived from the Jewish synagogue. The development of chant in the early Church was highly influenced by Greek, the common language of the Roman Empire, and likely adopted even by Jewish synagogues outside of Palestine. The nature of this chant was a melting pot of Jewish, Syrian, and Greek musical systems. Although Greek was the common language of the Eastern Roman Empire, and hence the language of the New Testament, Latin would eventually become the official liturgical language of the Western Church since it was already the literary and diplomatic standard of Rome in the early centuries of Christianity. Because Latin was common to the city of Rome and other regions of Italy, it may have also been spoken along with a vernacular dialect by the Roman army as it marched throughout the vast reaches of the empire.

Not sanctioned as part of the church liturgy was the use of musical instruments. The early Church fathers, including St. Augustine (354–430 A.D.), the

Bishop of Hippo and Doctor of the Church, were particularly appalled by such a prospect. In fact, they felt music was too seductive and might become a lure and end unto itself. The Church fathers' rejection of all musical instruments from Christian worship was also attributable to their association with pagan orgiastic rites and the barbarities of the Roman coliseum. Some Church elders wanted an outright ban on all music, but in their attempts to convert humanity to the Christian faith they were forced to concede that some music, which could be uplifting, should be allowed into the Church's official prayers in order to compete in the arena of souls. Most important, ancient people were accustomed to public speech, whether religious or political, being intoned or set to music pitches. This was particularly so in poetry, which was always sung.

The chants of the early Christian Church consisted mainly of psalms, the tones of which were clearly derived from synagogue practice, and the great canticles, i.e., hymns taken from the Bible, including *Nunc dimittis* (from Luke 2:29-32), *Magnificat* (from Luke 1:46-55), and *Benedictus* (from Luke 1:68-79). The singers were at first the Christian faithful, but by the fourth century, the chant repertoire was becoming complex enough to require trained singers, who were increasingly part of the clerical hierarchy, or choir monks in a monastery. They chanted these texts monophonically, i.e., in a single melodic line. For example, in the Ambrosian liturgy of Milan, the cantor would sing verses of the Psalms and Readings, and the congregation a simple refrain. In many places, the practice of women singing was frowned upon, because it was believed that men were readily aroused by the sounds of women's voices. In some regions, the congregation was split into two sections, the congregation and the choir, each singing verses of the Psalms, and eventually separate books for readers and the choir were compiled for use in the Mass and the Divine Office.

Concert

1st century A.D.
Roman mural
from Stabiae (near Pompeii)
Museo Archeologico
Nazionale, Naples

Consecration
of the Tabernacle
2nd century reconstructed
wall painting from
synagogue at Dura
Europus, Syria
Yale University Art Library

The celebration of the Eucharist, or the Mass, the essential core of Christian liturgical worship, was sung and the congregation joined in the singing, most likely in Greek. At churches as early as 130-135 A.D., the faithful sang the angels' hymn—the angelic salutation to the shepherds of Bethlehem: "Glory to God in the highest and on earth peace, good will to men." As Christmas evolved into a more celebrated feast day over the millennium, the clergy (especially monks) and lay people began composing their own Christmas hymns.

In addition to the Mass, monasteries, cathedrals, and some churches celebrated the Divine Office or Hours (meaning the official rites of the church), which consisted of eight sung liturgies throughout the day and night, whose core were the Psalms and New Testament canticles. The principal canonical hours were Matins, Lauds, Vespers, and Compline.

LATIN HYMNS

Latin hymns were songs of praise to God and part of the Divine Office, but not the Mass, and they expanded the church repertoire. The first metrical Latin hymns actually date from the late fourth century. Two of the earliest and most noteworthy compositions were *Jesus refulsit omnium* (Jesus, Light of All the Nations) by St. Hilary, the Bishop of Poitiers (c.315–368 A.D.), and *Veni redemptor gentium* (Come, Redeemer of Nations) by St. Ambrose, Bishop of Milan (c.340–397 A.D.). Highly esteemed by the Church, both bishops are regarded as the founders of Western church music, or Latin hymnody. Their metrical hymns were usually four-line stanzas in iambic tetrameter, and they served as the model for much Christian hymnody until the sixteenth century. These Latin hymns served as meditation and commentary on the biblical texts of the liturgy.

During the fourth century, coincidentally, the Feast of the Nativity was replacing the pagan rites of peasants throughout the Western world, from North Africa to Scandinavia, yet it is unlikely that the early hymns were composed for Christmas. The first Latin hymns in honor of the Nativity were written in the fifth century. They were more likely to be solemn and apt to emphasize the mystical nature of Christ's birth, such as the Christmas hymn *A solis ortus cardine* (From Lands That See the Sun Arise) by Caelius Sedulius (c.450 A.D.).

Latin hymns were being sung in cathedrals and monasteries by the latter part of the Middle Ages, especially during Advent in honor of the Nativity. Unfortunately, few members of the congregation, most of whom were illiterate, sang them since they were composed in Latin for choirs. Latin Nativity hymns became an important part of the Divine Office, and today they still remain an important aspect of the canonical hours of Christmastide.

Christian poets composed many of the Latin hymns from the time of St. Ambrose's death to the reign of Charlemagne. Most notable among them, besides Sedulius, were Aurelius Prudentius (348–c.413 A.D.), an official of the Roman government who penned *Corde natus ex parentis* (Of the Father's Love Begotten); Venantius Fortunatus (c.530–609 A.D.), later Bishop of Poitiers, who wrote *Agnoscat omne saeculum* (Let Every Age and Nation Know); and St. Isodore of Seville (c.560–636 A.D.), one of the last of the Christian Fathers.

From the fourth to tenth centuries, Latin hymns were rarely sung during the Mass, and the vocal participation of the worshippers declined as canonical choristers began to provide the musical response to the celebrant's chant. Choral music in the form of plainchant was an essential component of church services, and it was much encouraged by Pope Vitalian (657–672 A.D.).

Plainchant, also known as Gregorian chant, was monophonic, i.e., consisting of a single melodic line, originated in the oral tradition and was later systemized during the papacy of Gregory the Great (590–604 A.D.). This music-loving pontiff established the Roman *schola cantorum*, a specialized group of singers of church chant, and he instituted monastic chapters at all major basilicas, thus giving form to the Roman chant tradition. But these choirs were small in number, generally about ten to eighteen men and four to eight boys. Apart from convents, women were not allowed to participate in the *schola cantorum* or other church choirs.

With respect to liturgical hymns, many of the best of them were written from the ninth to the sixteenth century. St. Thomas Aquinas (c.1225–1274), the great theologian, was noted for hymns, particularly those commissioned by Pope Urban IV (c.1195–1264). His *Tantum ergo* (Down in Adoration Falling) was composed as a hymn for the then newly instituted Feast of Corpus Christi. Also included among the famous theologian's many works was *Panis angelicus* (Bread of Angels), a devotional hymn that is part of this sacred compilation.

Other noted theologians from the Middle Ages wrote sacred poems and contributed to the development of Latin hymns. They were Anselm of Canterbury (d.1109); scholastic Peter Abelard (d.1142); John Peckham, the Archbishop of

Canterbury (d.1292); and St. Bernard of Clairvaux (d.1153), a monastic theologian and proponent of pastoral care who authored hymns of mystic proportions. Noteworthy contributions were also made by Adam of St. Victor (active c.1170), an illustrious exponent of liturgical poetry and prolific hymn-writer from France; St. Bonaventure (1221–1274), doctor of the Church; and Thomas of Celano (active thirteenth century), an Italian Franciscan friar and biographer of Francis of Assisi, who composed the most famous Sequence of the Middle Ages—the *Dies irae* (Day of Wrath) of the Mass for the Dead, an awesome description of the Last Judgment.

Thomas of Celano's hymn, plus the *Stabat mater dolorosa* (The Sorrowful Mother Was Standing), a tender Latin hymn attributed to Jacopone da Todi (c.1230–1306), a widower turned mendicant friar, were two of the finest jewels in the Latin church repertoire. Today these two hymns still shine brilliantly amid many fine contributions made centuries later by the likes of St. Francis Xavier (d.1552), an important religious collaborator in the establishment of the Society of Jesus (the Jesuits); St. Teresa of Avila (1515–1582), founder of the Carmelite Order of nuns; John Henry Newman (1801–1890), eminent English church cardinal and theologian; and Frederick William Faber (1814–1863), English master in mystical theology.

LITURGICAL CHANT AND NOTATION

With the decline of congregational singing, Gregorian chant evolved as the official music of the Church. Pope Gregory I, also known as Gregory the Great, greatly increased the influence of Christendom. By the time of his election as pontiff, the language of the Roman Rite had largely converted from Greek to Latin. The sainted pope sought to bring conformity to the largely disorganized store of liturgical music, thus setting the stage for plainchant to be codified. Pope Gregory himself did not compose plainchant, although pious tradition gave him credit for it. It seems astonishing to us today, but monks and clerics committed the entire repertoires of chant to memory. It was not until the ninth century that manuscripts containing rudimentary notation were created, mainly to aid their failing collective memory.

With the blessing of Gregory the Great, plainchant gradually spread throughout Europe, as it had become an integral part of Roman Rite worship. However, after five centuries of Barbarian invasions, begun in the fifth century, and the eventual settlement of barbaric tribes among native peoples of the provinces of what was once part of the imperious Roman Empire, prospects for consolidation of liturgy and liturgical music were made more daunting. That was largely because of the negative impact the constant wars and invasions had on civilization, which was further exacerbated by the chaotic mingling of languages resulting from barbarian settlements. As a result of these incessant conflicts and forced mixture of languages, the development of various vernacular rites emerged in the West, although, as was the case for the early history of secular music, there is very little evidence from this span of the Dark Ages of any extant vernacular literature.

Despite the ascendancy of the Roman Rite and acceptance of Latin as the formal diplomatic and ecclesiastical language of the continent, achieving musical

St. Gregory
c. 870 illumination
from a Sacramentary fragment of Metz
School of Corbie
Bibliothèque Nationale de France, Paris

conformity and the supremacy of plainchant was still an immense and complicated process for the Church of Rome. Nevertheless, sometime during the seventh and eighth centuries the first books of the Western Rite, known as sacramentaries, appeared. These books of the Mass, generally incomplete compared to the more formalized Masses of later centuries, were either chanted or spoken by the priest celebrating the Mass. Sacramentaries also gave directions for movement and gestures called rubrics (meaning "red," the color ink they were written in); however, they contained no music for the choir.

Gregorian chant was evolving as a distinct form during this era of constant

conflict, and its ascendancy was made possible by the efforts of the Carolingians (614–1060), a Frankish noble family and the guardians of the Holy Roman Empire. The turning point for chant's ultimate acceptance, and indeed for the revival of civilization itself, came in the late eighth and early ninth centuries when Charlemagne (c.742–814), or, commonly, Charles the Great—a Carolingian and powerful Frankish king—resolved to reform and unify all Roman Church liturgy and liturgical music for his recently founded Holy Roman Empire. He was aided in his quest when on a visit to Rome he was crowned *Imperator Romanorum* (Emperor of the Romans) by Pope Leo III on Christmas Day in 800 A.D., his coronation presaging the revival of the Roman imperial tradition in the West. Charlemagne's inspiration first came about in his youth when his father, greatly impressed by the awesome majesty of the Roman Rite and its liturgical chant, sought and gained diplomatic relations with the Papacy. Soon after this development the Roman liturgy and chant, considered by both father and son as a way to contribute to civilization, were seriously promoted throughout the empire. Charlemagne's overall contributions to the people of Western Europe were invaluable, as he brought a sense of law and order and advanced Christianity, the arts, and civilization.

After Charlemagne's ascension to the throne, the Roman Rite eventually eclipsed all other Western liturgies, and plainchant (Gregorian chant) was exalted as the liturgical music standard for the Holy Roman Empire. With the unification of liturgy and church music, an objective long sought centuries earlier by Pope Gregory I and in whose name plainchant was defined, Gregorian chant was allowed to flourish and mature as the official music of the Roman Catholic Church, a distinction it would hold throughout the second millennium.

During the reign of Charlemagne and the ensuing centuries of the Middle Ages, the repertory of plainchant continued to greatly expand. Plainchant was monophonic music, meaning that no matter how many voices participated they all sang the same note, unsupported by harmony, although women and young boys sang an octave higher than men. Except in convents and schools, plainchant was sung only by male voices. In monasteries monks sang the prayers of the canonical hours, probably adopted from the Jewish practice of saying prayers seven times a day, and in parish churches canonical choristers sang at Mass and Vespers.

Over time, the repertory of plainchant had become so vast that it was difficult for singers to retain it. Thus it was necessary, indeed imperative, to develop some form of notational system by which certain parameters of music could be recorded. Because of the advancements in notation, composers were spared from having to memorize from the oral tradition the enormous repertoire of liturgy and chants. It was a remarkable feat for monks, choirmasters, musicians, and composers of the early Middle Ages to successfully retain and pass down such an immense amount of music, a task that had become more daunting with the constant additions to the liturgical repertoire. With the development of musical notation, which allowed for better transmission of complex liturgical compositions, plainchant became more exciting.

The importance of notation cannot be underestimated. Notation was largely

Charlemagne Crowned Emperor by Pope Leo III on December 25, 800 A.D. at St. Peter's in Rome
*c. 1455 illumination from Grandes chroniques de France
Jean Fouquet (c. 1420–1481), French
Bibliothèque Nationale de France, Paris*

influenced by educated monks and their preservation of precious music manuscripts. As it gradually developed from the seventh to ninth century in a modest form, a method of letter notation emerged. Symbols known as neumes, written above musical lines, indicated to singers which direction a note should move—up or down.

By the end of the ninth century, Gregorian chant had replaced most regional forms of chant. Because notation allowed for it to be written down, Gregorian chant became the first Western music that could be critically analyzed. The system of notation, in which lines and spaces specified the pitch of a note but not its rhythm, resulted from the contributions of many liturgical composers over the ages.

Notation became more codified about 1040 in the writings of Guido of Arezzo (c.991–c.1050), an Italian theorist, music teacher, and Benedictine monk. Guido used a teaching device that helped students visualize and memorize the notes of the hexachord (a six-note segment of a scale). Guido was acclaimed for his techniques of teaching sight singing, or reading a piece of music without having seen it before. He reputedly invented solmization, whereby he assigned each tone of the hexachord to the first syllable of each verse of a famous musical piece dedicated to St. John the Baptist. These musical notes were named *ut* (later changed to *do), re, mi, fa, sol,* and *la,* the first syllables of each half-line from *"Ut queant laxis,"* the plainchant hymn to St. John the Baptist composed earlier by Paulus Diaconus (c.720–799) another Benedictine monk and noted historian of the Lombards. Notice the underlined first syllable on each line of the plainchant hymn:

LATIN	ENGLISH
1. *Ut queant laxis*	That your servants
2. *Resonare fibris*	May freely sing
3. *Mira gestorum*	The miracles
4. *Famuli tuorum*	Of your deeds
5. *Solve poluti*	Remove all stains [of sin]
6. *Labii reatum, Sancte Ioannes!*	From their unclean lips, Saint John!

Most important, Guido developed the musical staff of four lines (a fifth was added later by an anonymous composer) that enabled his choirboys to learn in a few days what had previously taken them many weeks. For this invention he has earned the title *inventor musicae.*

During Guido's time the musical repertoire of church liturgy was extraordinarily large and highly advanced. The music in church was no longer sung by the people but by the trained clerics, monks, and all-male choirs, a development easily understood because most professional musicians of the Middle Ages were employed by the Church. Much of the Gregorian chant needed for the whole church year was contained in massive manuscript books, such as the *Antiphonale missarum* (Gradual for the Mass chants), Kyrie chants, and the *antiphonale* (for the Divine Office chants). Special chants reserved for soloists and the arrangement of chants by modal similarities for easier memorization and reading constituted the entire Gregorian chant repertoire. Gregorian chant, one might remember, was assembled for musical and liturgical conformity, and the Church had intended to keep it unchanged.

However, musical practice, at least in Western civilization, had not remained static and unchanged, and many influences, including secular ones, forced an evolution of style. With the advancement of musical notation, liturgical music composers were freed from the tremendous burden of having to memorize all the liturgical texts. No longer so burdened, musicians began to experiment and compose additions to the texts and melodies, thereby embellishing the rigidity of the standard repertoire.

These additions of words to an already existing text or melody were called tropes, and they were usually limited to ten notes. As church services became more elaborate and longer from the tenth to thirteenth century, the composition of tropes helped to meet the demands for more music not provided by the standard repertoire. Tropes adorned Gregorian chant for the Propers and the Ordinary of the Mass, giving birth to whole new books of responsory prayers and antiphons (devotional compositions sung responsively as part of a liturgy) to serve such occasions.

Guido d'Arezzo with His Pupil Archbishop Theodaldus
12th century illumination from a treatise on music
Oesterreichische
Nationalbibliothek, Vienna

POLYPHONY AND SECULAR MUSIC

Since music could be notated, the rise of collections of polyphonic compositions soon followed. Polyphony—from the Greek for "many sounds"—consisted of a combination of more than one independent voice parts with a chant melody, more like a harmony with contrasting voices. In the seventh and eighth centuries the rudimentary elements of polyphony were practiced in oral and unwritten tradition. By the tenth century, polyphonic music was maturing as a musical force able to compete with monophonic religious chant.

Although liturgical polyphony was used mostly as settings for the Ordinary and the Propers of the Mass, it also allowed for arrangements of Latin hymns, sung at various church services, to become some of the most beautiful and moving sentiments of medieval times. This is understandable, since music in the Middles Ages was largely influenced by the Church's dictates and as a result composers acceded to its liturgical requirements. The history of these hymns, thought to have begun with St. Ambrose of Milan and Bishop Hilary of Poitiers, as noted earlier, flourished under the influence of Moslem and Provencal love poetry, giving Latin hymns a depth of great feeling and delicacy.

The rise of polyphony was also accompanied by the rise of secular songs. Most of these secular songs were about love and all of its emotions. In the countries of Christendom, troubadours and minstrels composed their own poems, setting them to music as they traveled the countryside, or journeyed on long pilgrimages, such as the Crusades. In this way, they contributed to the advancement of secular songs.

Troubadours were generally of noble birth and more cultivated than minstrels; the latter were considered professional entertainers from the lower classes. In the Middle Ages, or the medieval period, these wandering poets, including the *minnesingers* of Germany and the *trovatori* of Italy, who shared the same social plateau as the troubadours of France, were quite popular. Most of the poetry written before the thirteenth century was meant to be sung, generally in monophonic melodies, by the individual itinerant musician; however, in some instances where it was not accepted practice to sing other people's music, that music was lost because it was not notated. Perhaps the most famous of all troubadours was Adam de la Halle (c.1237–c.1286), who composed one of the oldest secular music pieces for theater titled *Le jeu de Robin et Marion.*

The secular flavor of the new poetry and song germinated in Provence, a southern region of France, where it was quite pronounced and where poems and songs were essentially sung for the nobility. Lyrics could be about love, drinking, parodies of liturgical texts, the Crusades, or other subjects. Around 1080 the impact of this secular art of France spread to other parts of Europe; nonetheless, its life span was brief, since that music, too, was monophonic. As interest in polyphony increased, especially in noble circles and in some quarters of the Church in the early thirteenth century, the amateur poet-musicians, or troubadours, received considerably less attention.

The flowering of polyphony occurred at the Cathedral of Notre Dame in Paris during the twelfth century, when church services continued to become more elaborate and longer. The composition of tropes, i.e., the addition of words as an embellishment to the text of the Mass or Divine Office to be sung by a choir, helped to meet the demands for more music not provided by the standard church repertoire. Since Paris was acknowledged as the musical center of the Western world and its university one of the first to include the theoretical study of music as part of its curriculum, it was natural for the choir school of Notre Dame to further advancements

A Troubadour
*14th century manuscript
illumination
from* Livre des cent ballades,
*by Jean le Sénéchal
(French School)
Musée Condé, Chantilly, France*

in music. Included among them was *organum*, an important stage in polyphony's development that was fostered by Leonin (active c.1163–1190) and Pérotin (active c.1200), two important composers in medieval Paris.

Organum was an early form of melodic harmonization for two independent voices in a polyphonic setting, and was one of the most important achievements of the Notre Dame school. There further development of polyphony by the notation of rhythmic modes, i.e. six metrical patterns was highly encouraged. Thus arrangements for Gregorian chant were of a grand scale and style, designed exclusively for trained singers, both soloists and choirs, although improvised at first and notated later. The medieval penchant for layering of meanings and

Etienne Chevalier and His Patron Paying Homage to the Virgin and Child
15th century manuscript illumination
Jean Fouquet (c. 1420–1481), French
Musée Condé, Chantilly, France

theological elaboration expressed itself in the continued practice of troping. Organum, which is essentially a kind of polyphonic trope, led to the creation of motets.

The motet is a short unaccompanied (no instruments) sacred choral composition designed for trained singers, both soloists and choirs, in which three, four, five, or even six different voices are sung in a complex weave of individual melodies. With the introduction of the motet, Gregorian chant was made more glorious in polyphonic Mass settings. Fine examples of this type of choral composition composed in later centuries are the highly devotional *Hodie Christus natus est* by Jan Pieterszoon Sweelinck (1562-1621), an eminent Dutch composer, and *Hört zu ihr lieben Leute* by Michael Praetorius (1571-1621), the prolific German music scholar.

By the fourteenth century the motet moved away from its church roots as its audience, the members of the nobility, was becoming more secular and receptive to the madrigal, a secular equivalent of the motet that was not subject to the restrictions that prevailed in church music. It was also an age when the secularization of all the arts had become more pronounced; and when paintings and sculptures and other forms of visual art were less devoted to strictly religious themes, a trend that has continued unabated up to and beyond the twentieth century.

The fourteenth century was also a time of social upheaval and real troubles for the Church. Because of the influence of the Avignon Papacy (1305–1378), in which a series of seven popes resided in France instead of at the Vatican in Rome, followed by the Great Church Schism (1378–1415), and various abuses by the clergy—the failure to observe vows and its overt engagement in worldly pleasures, the Church could no longer count on total allegiance from its subjects. In the sphere of music, this disengagement led to the composition of more secular music, the inspiration for which was found in the non-liturgical world. This new spirit was captured and condensed by Philippe de Vitry (1291–1361), a French churchman, in his 1322 treatise *Ars nova,* meaning "new art."

The *Ars nova* is most notable for its achievements in the area of rhythm. The rhythmic practices of the fourteenth century, in fact, reached a complexity that would not be seen again until the second half of the twentieth century. In many instances the early compositions of the *Ars nova* showed a lack of purpose, indicative of an age when too much attention was directed to the intricacies of the new art form and when the distinction between sacred and secular music was deliberately blurred.

The influence of the French *Ars nova* was particularly felt in Italy during the early part of the fourteenth century. Even there, most polyphonic compositions were largely secular. Nevertheless, some of the liturgical compositions of the period were exceptional in their grandeur, particularly the *Messe de Nostre Dame* by Guillaume de Machaut (1300–1377), one of the most famous medieval pieces of sacred music. The most celebrated composer of the fourteenth century, Machaut was the first to write a cohesive and complete polyphonic setting of the Ordinary of the Mass.

With the passage of time, the use of instruments to replace or double vocal parts became common practice. The new trend, coupled with secular music's invasion of the ecclesiastical sphere, caused bitter complaints from members of the clergy, and Gregorian chant continued to be eclipsed by the new music. Because of the dissolution of the monasteries in England by King Henry the VIII in the sixteenth century, during which period many of earlier church music manuscripts were destroyed, there is little evidence that musicians in England kept up with the innovations of the French and Italian *Ars nova*. The works of John Dunstable (1390–1453), one of the first great English composers, who probably wrote the first instrumental accompaniment for church music, survived the dissolution and they were highly acclaimed on the Continent. Dunstable's simpler music style accentuating smoother-flowing melodies was emulated by the composers of Burgundy, France, and became characteristic of the early Renaissance. During this same era, French composer, Guillaume Dufay (c.1400–1474), was being highly acclaimed for his melodic clarity and expressive tunes. His surviving works include eighty-four songs, eight Masses, and his 1436 masterpiece for the consecration of Santa Maria del Fiore, the famous Florentine cathedral.

Another musical titan, Josquin Desprez (c.1440–1521), was also being recognized for his creative genius. His motets and polyphonic Masses produced a musical style that was emulated on the Continent by other important composers of sacred polyphony, especially those from France and the Netherlands. Characteristics of this style were simplicity in choral writing and a resulting clarity of text, or "word painting," i.e., an attempt to depict actual words through music. Although Josquin wrote highly organized and complex music, he did not set out to express emotional reaction to or word painting of the text. His works existed in their perfection, constructed like a great cathedral with innovative notes that soar to the highest naves.

These musical innovations furthered the acceptance of polyphony in both the ecclesiastical and secular realms. And it was during the early stages of the Renaissance that original Christmas carol compositions appeared and when a variety of musical instruments brought flavor to both church and secular music. Most of these instruments were of Oriental origin, except for the keyboard.

THE ADVENT OF CAROLS

With notation firmly established and the dawning of the Renaissance, the rise of secular compositions continued unabated. Some of these compositions included carols. Although many carols were religious in content, they were essentially non-liturgical in nature. Carols originally came from secular and pagan sources. The Greeks sung them in their plays, and the Romans used them during Saturnalia, their major festival. They were quite popular and sung for weddings, birthdays, and other festivities.

The word *carol* may have been derived from a number of sources, including the Greek word *charos,* the Anglo-Saxon word *kyrriole,* medieval dances called *carolles* or *karolles,* or the French word *carole.* Originally the word carol meant a round dance. In later years it would be defined as a joyful religious song, and it is in this context by which Christmas carols are best known. Today most people think of carols as strictly Christmas songs, and it is estimated that at least four to five thousand carols exist, most of them in the realm of the obscure.

The origin of carols cannot be understood without a linkage to dancing. Just like singing in the early Church, dancing had been frowned upon by church authorities because they considered it immoral and associated it with heathen worship. But long before the birth of Christianity, dancing and singing had existed together in religious festivals. The Romans had religious dances, as did the Druids and other religious priesthoods, and eventually these dances found their way into the Christian Church. Dancing, however, would become outlawed in church after some scandals. The Council of Toledo in 589 and the Council of Avignon in 1209 would separately ban dancing entirely from church worship. But in the countryside of England and Europe it was common practice to sing carols, both religious and secular, and dance at the same time.

The modern definition of *carol* is probably best defined by Percy Dearmer (1867–1936), co-author of *The Oxford Book of Carols,* a compilation published in 1928. He described the carol as a song with a religious impulse that is simple, hilarious, popular, and modern. A carol is folk-like in character. It is simple, has little pretense to it, has plain lyrics, and is a seasonal song. From the early fourteenth century until the outset of the Reformation, the carol was defined as a poem suitable for singing, made up of uniform stanzas, and provided with a burden, or an external refrain, repeated after each stanza.

The first carol, according to legend, was actually a hymn sung by angels appearing to the shepherds of Bethlehem and declaring the birth of Christ with the words *"Gloria in excelsis Deo"* and "peace to men of good will." Yet very few vernacular carols were known prior to the fourteenth century owing to the predominance of church liturgy and Latin.

By the twentieth century carols had become an indispensable part of the Christmas music repertoire. This was made possible because of improved methods of musical transmission, notably the invention of notation, the rise of secular music, and the eventual domination of the vernacular tongue in the composition of songs, among which were carols.

KEYBOARD INSTRUMENTS

Besides notation, the invention of the keyboard instrument was a critical development in the world of Western music. The keyboard allowed a performer to play many different notes at the same time. This was a significant factor in the advance of more exciting and creative polyphonic instrumental works from the sixteenth century onward.

The organ, whose creation provided the first really serious competitor to the human voice, was the keyboard instrument most associated with church liturgy. Dating several centuries before the birth of Christ, the organ was not held in high esteem by church officials in the early days of Christianity because it was associated with pagan Roman entertainment and the slaughter of Christians in the Roman amphitheater. From the end of the fifth century until the middle of the eighth century, there is little evidence that the organ was known in the West. In the eighth century it was re-introduced to the Western world, and by the ninth

A Carole in the Orchard
from Le Roman de la rose
c. 1460 French illuminated manuscript
Bibliothèque Nationale de France, Paris

century it was part of the cultural life of Europe. By the tenth century the organ was an important aspect of Christian worship, and near the end of the Middle Ages organs of a grander size were being built in many cathedrals and abbey churches throughout Europe and England.

The organ was the first instrument with a keyboard, originally played with the fists because the keys were so large. But as is the case with most technologies, improvement was on the way. Important keyboard innovations and inventions were subsequently introduced to the world of music, including the clavichord, harpsichord, and ultimately the pianoforte (piano).

The clavichord was the keyboard innovation of the twelfth century. By the sixteenth century the harpsichord was the most important keyboard instrument in use, variants of which were the virginals and spinet in England, the latter of which was also popular in Italy, until the piano came into prominence by the late eighteenth century.

Since the late sixteenth century, keyboard instruments have greatly influenced the music of Western civilization, and the organ was as highly

left

**The Organ as Symbol of
the Church**

*from Thomas a Kempis,
Liber interne consolacionis,
early 15th century
English miniature
British Library, London*

right

**Angels Playing Musical
Instruments**

*c. 1487–1490 oil on right panel
of triptych
Hans Memling (c. 1433–1494),
German-Flemish
Koninklijk Museum voor
Schone Kunsten, Antwerp,
Belgium*

developed as it is today. The advancement of these keyboard instruments was
critical because it allowed solo performers to study and perform polyphonic
music. Polyphony, one might recall, was an important improvement on monophonic singing—a solo vocal style distinguished by having a single melodic line
and instrumental accompaniment—that had dominated music for so many
centuries.

Other instruments in use during the Renaissance period were plucking
instruments, such as the lute, harp, citterns (pear-shaped guitars), psalteries, dul-
cimers, and guitars; fiddling instruments, such as the viol of various sizes and the
violin (developed in Italy and popular there); wind instruments, such as flutes,
fifes (pipes), recorders, shawms, sackbuts, bagpipes, trumpets, horns, and oboes;
and percussion instruments, such as drums, cymbals, tambourines, and castanets.
Musical instruments, including bagpipes, appeared often as illustrations in manuscripts of the age.

These instruments were subordinated to the voice since the great virtuosos
of the Renaissance were singers. Performances by several instruments in concert

were given and supported by aristocratic patronage. By the sixteenth century the development of music no longer relied on the Church for its greatest support. Great experimentation and diversity of vocal and instrumental compositions had already been made in secular music of the Renaissance era. The influence of the Church, moreover, had continued to seriously wane with respect to matters of the soul, not to mention music and songs.

With the ushering in of the Age of Reformation (1517–1564), a whole new dynamic was reshaping the religious landscape of Christian Europe. The history of this change would also affect Christmas and its music.

THE REFORMATION

Martin Luther (1483–1546), a German monk and leader of the Reformation, was a lover of German music and folk songs. He felt that the church liturgy was too aristocratic and had become too detached from the common people. This detachment was embodied in the Church's practice of isolating the priest and all male choir who sang the Mass away from the worshippers.

Luther sought reforms in music, as he sought change in theology, ethics, ritual, and art. He loved polyphony and wanted music that moved people by fusing faith and song. He encouraged a greater participation by the congregation in singing, and he simplified the music from choir plainsong to easy harmony, thus reducing the role and influence of the Mass. Toward this end, Luther published hundreds of hymn texts to be sung to popular melodies and simple chants.

In the sixteenth and seventeenth centuries, the Reformation extended the range of religious choral music beyond the liturgy, and the informal group singing of songs was highly encouraged, leading to a greater familiarity with Christmas hymns. Some founders of other Protestant sects, especially Calvinists, did not like the idea of music being played at all in church, much like the Fathers of the early Christian Church, and they put limits on the amount of music that could be played. Their restrictions also led to a sharp reduction of boisterous observances of Christmas, and they were more likely to welcome psalm settings or other scriptural texts. The singing of joyful hymns or carols, even those that adhered to scriptural meaning, were frowned upon.

Polyphony, on the other hand, made extraordinary advancements during the eras of the late Renaissance and the Reformation. French and Flemish composers brought new color and ornamentation to the ever-increasing musical technique. In Spain, music was marked by an exceptional piety and mysticism as a result of a confluence of Moorish, Italian, French, and Flemish music, an excellent example of which was *O magnum mysterium* by Tomás Luis de Victoria (1548–1611), one of the greatest Spanish composers of the late Renaissance.

The advancement of polyphony was considerably aided by the use of choir books throughout the Middle Ages and Renaissance. Choral manuscripts, which enhanced church liturgy and the singing of the Divine Office, were necessary to accommodate the ever-increasing demand for elaborate church music. Many choral books were large enough to be placed on lecterns, thereby allowing both choirmaster and members of the choir to view them simultaneously. What made these

choral books especially prized manuscripts, besides their practical use, were their spectacular illuminations of decorated letters, often embellished with rich pigments and gold leaf and drawn large enough to contain biblical scenes and sacred figures.

By the sixteenth century, the elaborate sacred polyphony for the Ordinary of the Mass had gone far beyond its original intent as the paraphrasing of Gregorian chant became widespread. This phenomenon, known as the Parody Mass (better defined as an "Imitation Mass," since there was no humor involved), was so elaborate that original church plainchant was almost unrecognizable. Many sixteenth-century composers, nevertheless, favored the Parody Mass, usually based on secular chansons (songs), some of which could be bawdy, that characteristically combined several melodies in a polyphonic texture. More often than not, though, secular chansons formed the basis for the Parody Mass.

Another notable development of the period was the Organ Mass, in which verses were performed alternately by the organ and sung plainchant or polyphony. But the human voice was destined to be replaced by musical instruments alone. Until the fifteenth century nearly all compositions that included instruments doubled or replaced single-line voices and were considered equal, but composers of polyphonic instrumental works changed the musical landscape in the sixteenth century. They began to compose strictly for instruments, mostly in the form of keyboard music that embellished or replaced song, because of the growth in sophistication of village and courtly traditions of instrumental dance music.

CHURCH ACCEPTANCE OF POLYPHONY

By the sixteenth century the development of music no longer relied on the Church for its greatest support, since the great diversity of vocal and instrumental compositions came from the secular music realm of the Renaissance. Despite the turbulence of the Reformation that only added to its woes, the Catholic Church still held considerable influence on music and the arts because of its patronization. No other religious organization contributed more in both finances and moral support. From the Middle Ages to the late sixteenth century the Roman Mass was the primary vehicle by which a music composer could demonstrate his craft. Even among Protestants the highest and most admired form of musical composition was the Mass, and Protestant choirs were likely to imitate the Catholic pattern.

The polyphonic music of the late sixteenth century was quite distinguished as composers began to search for yet more perspective in their music. Gone were the days of the customary three-voice parts that had expanded into four a century earlier. In the new era five-and six-voice parts had become standard and more dramatic. Some sacred works went beyond six voices, such as *Ecce beatam lucem,* a motet written by Alessandro Striggio (c.1536–1592), an Italian Renaissance composer, for an astonishing ten four-part choirs, or forty voices, and incredibly doubled by instruments! Striggio's impressive work for a Bavarian royal marriage may have inspired Thomas Tallis (c.1505–1575), one of England's great Renaissance composers, to produce his own forty-voice tour-de-force, a motet known as *Spem in alium* for the imperial Queen Elizabeth I (1533–1603), the last of the Tudor monarchs.

But it may have been Giovanni Luigi Palestrina (1526–1594), a preeminent composer of his day, who may have helped to win a permanent place and acceptance of polyphonic music inside the Church. His famous *Missa papae marcelli* was supposedly offered to Pope Pius IV (1499–1565) in an effort to prevent polyphonic music from being banned from the liturgy. Although Palestrina's contribution has been unsubstantiated and was not noted in the official record of the Council of Trent (1545–1563), one that nearly banned outright any playing of music inside churches because of the incursion of secular music in the liturgy, his music probably held sway with the papacy and within clerical circles. This would have been especially true for those church officials who were particularly offended by some of the parody Masses making ancient liturgical chant almost unintelligible. Church officials who deigned to listen to Palestrina's sacred works may have found enlightenment about the possibilities of including them in Mass celebrations, thus forsaking the strict standard of only using monophonic settings of ancient chant in the Mass.

BAROQUE FULFILLMENT

The Baroque period of music (1600–1750) was witness to the full flower of the *concertato* style in instrumental music and the growth of the chorale, the latter heavily influenced by Martin Luther's ideas about church music. The concertato style, derived from *concert,* for seventeenth century music, involved elements of contrast whereby melody is shared between several different voices in a performance. The development of the violin as a virtuoso musical instrument fulfilled the possibilities of the new Baroque compositions. Especially sought after were violins made by the Amati family and Antonius Stradivarius (1644–1737). Their finely crafted violins, still highly coveted by serious musicians and collectors, are now considered priceless.

Out of the Venetian *concerto grosso* came the more modern idea of the concerto as a musical form in which a solo instrument is pitted against the resources of a whole orchestra. The concertato style was epitomized by the Italian compositions of the period, an excellent example of which was the *Concerto Grosso in G Minor, Op.6/8* by Arcangelo Corelli (1653–1713), one of the truly great masters of that musical style. His creative opus, also known as "Christmas Concerto," was widely admired by musicians throughout Europe and together with his other eleven concerto pieces demonstrated the beauty of the Italian concertato style.

One of the musical forerunners of the Italian concerto composers was Heinrich Schütz (1585–1672), a very religious man and perhaps the greatest German composer of the seventeenth century. Schütz emulated the polychoral technique of the Venetian composers, Andrea and Giovanni Gabrieli, who dedicated their best efforts to the motet rather than the Mass by composing for single, double, or triple choirs, each one supported by an organ or an instrumental group. However, Schütz took the secular madrigal style of Germany and applied it to sacred music before incorporating the elaborate instrumentation of the Venetians. Schütz, who composed music for a variety of vocal and instrumental combinations, was the standard-bearer of a musical form and spirit that some years later would find perfection in the compositions of Johann Sebastian Bach (1685–1750) and George Frederic Handel (1685–1759).

Schütz's fellow countryman, Michael Praetorius (1571–1621), was also busy at his craft, compiling large tomes of music and writing his *Syntagma musicum*, a thorough and scholarly encyclopedia of musical history, instruments, and forms. Praetorius, a composer of exceptional motets, was also noted for his harmonization of German carols.

During Schütz's lifetime other events and musicians emerged. In 1630 the great basilica of St. Peter's in Rome was finally dedicated after 176 years of massive construction. Churches in Italy reverberated with Masses, vespers, motets, and toccatas rolled from organs that had reached their golden age of creation. Choirs of men and boys, the latter singing soprano parts, along with the voices of specially trained monks, filled the naves with glorious polyphony.

BACH AND HANDEL

By the seventeenth century, "modern" notation was solidly established, an important development for the more sophisticated and creative composer. In Europe the legacy of the seventeenth-century Baroque blossomed with the works of Johann Sebastian Bach (1685–1750) and George Frideric Handel (1685–1759). And during the lifetimes of these two musical giants of the high Baroque period a strictly independent instrumental style of music flourished.

Opera, or the theater, however, dominated all the music of the Baroque. Created around 1600 by the Florentine Camarata, an intellectual society of noblemen who attempted to recreate the music of the Greek theater, and promoted by Claudio Monteverdi (1567–1643), a Venetian composer and musical innovator best known for his secular works, opera was the first art music that appealed to a large audience, and in return it began to reflect growing popular tastes. Monteverdi was so greatly admired, and such was his innate musical talent to express emotion and drama in vocal music, that it was known for people to weep during the performance of his operatic arias. As a result of the popularity of these musical dramas, mostly based on stories from classical mythology and traditional romances, the first opera house was opened in Venice in 1637.

Contemporaries of Monteverdi preferred the use of solo voices for operatic performances to express the dramatic import they believed was inherent in ancient Greek drama. These developments saw the introduction of solo arias in motets, which at the time meant music set to a sacred Latin text. This secular spillage into the sacred realm meant Mass music was expanded into a larger form consisting of independent choruses and arias combined with instrumental movements. Some of the changes, however, constituted liturgical abuse, i.e., the liturgy was suppressed by the new art music, causing alarm in religious circles.

Within Lutheran Church circles, the chorale, or congregational hymn, was often an integral element of sacred compositions, particularly sacred cantatas. Perfected by Bach and his contemporaries, the chorale added to the glory of Baroque music, and during their era the oratorio attained its highest development. Bach's *St. Matthew Passion*, the *Christmas Oratorio*, and *Mass in B Minor* have been thought, by some authorities, to be among the greatest compositions in the history of Western music, although Handel's *Messiah* is the more popular and famous piece that is much performed during the Christmas season.

The contributions of Bach and Handel exemplified the tender sentiment and massive piety that Germans poured into their works for organ music and chorales. The oratorio, which was taken up early in the seventeenth century by the Jesuits in their efforts to re-establish the power of the Roman Church and to stem the powerful tides of secularization sweeping through Europe, was perfected by the Lutheran Bach and by Handel, the German-born English composer. The fervor of Protestantism inspired both Baroque giants and other composers to write many cantatas, chorales, and passions.

A Gothic Protestant Church
1685 oil on canvas
Emanuel De Witte
(c. 1616–1692), Dutch
The State Hermitage Museum,
St. Petersburg, Russia

Johann Sebastian Bach
Playing and Conducting
in Concert in 1714 in the
Chapel Choir of Weimar
engraving, after a painting by
H. W. Schmidt
(active late 18th century),
German Lebrecht Music & Arts
Photo Library, London

The Lutheran Church embellished the Passion narratives with a special chant, punctuating the chant with polyphonic settings of the text. Some church composers then set out to incorporate texts modeled from opera segments, discarding all biblical references and hymn texts for poetical passages. This caused problems for Lutheran elders. Bach used some of these textual techniques while retaining complete biblical texts, incorporating chorales, choruses, and arias of a non-scriptural nature into his *Christmas Oratorio*. Handel's *Messiah* also illustrates the strong influence of late seventeenth-century Italian opera on his music.

The Baroque period was the age of polyphonic fulfillment. The orchestra had already been in use for choir and the opera, especially in the latter's overtures, a significant development during the latter stages of the seventeenth century. Most composers of Italian opera relished the opportunity to create instrumental music for opera overtures as opposed to pandering to the sometimes harsh and fickle demands of opera singers. Writing overtures allowed them to display talents in purely orchestral form, which theretofore may have gone unnoticed.

On the European Continent, polyphonic keyboard music that began its rise in France during the early seventeenth century had by the eighteenth century reached its apotheosis in Germany. By the end of the eighteenth century, many of the fine Italian Baroque concertos had already been performed, and the dawning of the Classical era was at hand. As result of this new development, the stage was set for the next level of musical achievement—the symphony. And on the horizon loomed Haydn and Mozart.

THE CLASSICAL ERA

Joseph Haydn (1732–1809), one of the great Viennese composers, as well as Carl Philipp Emmanuel Bach (1714–1788), noted son of Johann Sebastian Bach, would help to usher in the new sacred music. Even Haydn's brother, Michael Haydn (1737–1806), composed numerous religious works, including sixty-five *offertoriums* (Offertories of the Mass), one of which was *Anima nostra* (Our Soul) for a Christmastide Mass commemorating the slaughter of the innocents of Bethlehem. It was also the age of Wolfgang Amadeus Mozart (1756–1791), the titan in the pantheon of Viennese classical musicians, who would be feted in the royal courts of Austria, first for his genius and virtuosity,

Interior of the Choir in the Capuchin Church on the Piazza Barberini in Rome
1820 oil on canvas
Francois Marius Granet
(1775–1849), French
The State Hermitage Museum, St. Petersburg, Russia

and secondly for instrumental music and operas. His ability to craft beautiful melody was unsurpassed, and his ability to incorporate the sonata form (a musical composition played on instruments as opposed to being sung) in vocal music was entirely new.

The interests of Viennese composers were in formal structures and the melodic and harmonic freedoms of opera and the cantata. Although this new music often was more instrumental and theatrical than religious, church composers incorporated these new melodies into liturgical texts. The sonata form and its incorporation into symphonic music proved more dramatic and emotional than earlier examples, even dominating the composition of Masses and other important liturgical texts. As a result of these new developments, there was no clear division in style between sacred and secular music.

The sheer volume of works by both Joseph Haydn and Mozart demonstrate the level of influence they had on the advancement of music; in fact, the combined output of these two great Austrian composers is considered the apogee of the Classical era. Haydn produced highly esteemed works in both the religious and secular music world. His sacred pieces included cantatas, oratorios, and many fine sung Masses, especially his last six Mass compositions, written in the late 1790s and early 1800s for the Esterhazy family. He wrote some of the finest symphonies, string quartets, and keyboard sonatas, taking them to heights never achieved before, and ultimately earning him the distinction of having mastered all the existing musical forms of the classical repertoire.

Mozart, on the other hand, only devoted a small fraction of his genius toward liturgical compositions; his great loves were opera, sonata, symphony, and concerto. But when Mozart did employ his creative energy to sacred composition, he produced very fine and finished music of the liturgy for the Saltzburg Cathedral, including Masses, motets, vespers, and litanies. His sacred works, including the famous unfinished *Requiem,* combined polyphonic choir and the symphony orchestra in a logical and balanced form that produced expressive melody. Mozart's contributions in the realm of sacred music, along with those of Joseph Haydn, came at a time when Joseph II of Austria (1741–1790), known as the "music king," decreed the restoration of liturgical propriety in his attempt to encourage better congregational worship.

These classical composers were considerably aided by the pianoforte, or piano, an important keyboard instrument invented almost a century earlier by Bartolomeo Cristofori di Francesco (1655–1731). With its growing range and power, the piano further freed music from the shackles of words, and as a result instrumental music began to greatly outstrip vocal works in volume and scale.

SACRED MUSIC ENDURES

After the death of Mozart and Haydn, the incomparable Ludwig van Beethoven (1770–1827) helped to carry on the classical style. Along with Franz Schubert (1797–1828), another Austrian composer of renown, Beethoven created memorable works in symphony, sonatas, and string quartets. The contributions of Schubert, however, broached the realm of Romanticism, as his songs tended to stir the emotional impulse.

Sacred Music
1841 oil on canvas
Luigi Mussini (1813–1888),
Italian (Florentine)
Galleria dell' Accademia,
Florence

In the world of instrumental music, the death of Johannes Brahms (1833–1897) marked the end of a 212-year period dominated by German music. Since the birth of Bach and Handel in 1685, most of the greatest living composers were of the German tongue. Fifty years earlier, another German master, Felix Mendelssohn (1809–1847), had passed from the world of music. His last work was an unfinished Christmas composition titled *Christus oratorio*.

But it was Italian and French composers who were predominant forces in the realms of secular and sacred music during this same period. From France came a number of great composers, including César Franck, a peerless organist who wrote the inspiring music for St. Thomas Aquinas's prayer *Panis angelicus*. Other sacred works of the nineteenth century represented the influence of Romantic symphonic music that would find expression in concerted Masses. More often than not, however, the composer was more concerned about musical effect that was likely to be secular or sentimental. These concerted Masses were therefore objectionable on liturgical grounds since they distracted the congregation from the action of the Mass. By the same token, some were treasured as Catholic-inspired music and highly suited for concert performances outside of liturgy.

Although music for any period possesses elements of romance, the period from 1820 to 1900 was accentuated by emotional and picturesque music that appeared to depend less on formal structures. Romantic music in the nineteenth century was particularly evident in grandiose operas and music dramas. French, German, and Italian composers made significant contributions to the genre. Their operas provided for highly emotional scenes and a stage for spectacular singing, particularly the *bel canto,* or "beautiful singing," of the Italians, a movement begun in the late 1700s or early 1800s. The opera was the most suitable outlet for nineteenth-century artistic expression that valued sentimental love, emotional and violent conflict, dramas about human relationships, and, in some instances, comedy or grand mythological tales, the latter being the expressive domain of German composer Richard Wagner (1813–1883).

During the nineteenth century, Protestant church music assumed a variety of forms. The oratorio, less popular then in Catholic countries, was still performed, particularly at Christmas and Easter services. Choral music for the Mass was part of the celebration of the Eucharist by the other traditional denominations, the Lutherans and Anglicans (Episcopalians in America). Excellent hymns were written, or newly discovered, in England. European, English, and American composers were inspired by folk music idioms. Americans contributed a more rugged type of hymn and black spirituals, as well as wholly original English-language Christmas carols. These contributions of hymns and carols, plus original sacred music scored for ancient prayers, whether Latin or vernacular (see "The Lord's Prayer" on page 82) continued well into the twentieth century, a period when harmony and rhythm further distinguished the individuality of the composer.

For the Catholic Church, one of the most significant achievements of the nineteenth century was a religious revival that helped with the restoration of Gregorian chant. It was a monumental task undertaken by the Benedictine monks of Solesmes, France, who had persuaded Pope Pius IX (1846–1878) in 1870 to grant them permission to launch the effort. The scholarship of the Solesmes monks was further approved by Pope Pius X (1903–1914) in 1903, when he pronounced Gregorian chant and Renaissance polyphony as the official style of Catholic Church music.

In the twentieth century, the trend toward versatility in the religious repertoire, keeping in mind the sensitivities of church elders and their preferred musical tastes, was accelerated by the reforms of the Vatican II Council of the 1960s. Usage of the vernacular language was officially approved in church ritual, and as a result the Catholic Church repertoire was less about Latin and more about local language hymns.

Although less conservative than their predecessors in views about music, the Catholic Church hierarchy and many of its faithful, however, still maintained affection for its Latin heritage. This affection was manifested in July of 2007, when Pope Benedict XVI issued a papal directive allowing for a greater use of the Tridentine (or Latin) Mass. Even though sanctioned on a limited and non-exclusive basis, the pontiff's action reaffirmed the Catholic Church's ancient liturgical tradition, and by inference its great polyphonic heritage.

THE MUSIC PROGRAM

Against this historic backdrop, the selections for *Sacred Christmas Music* has been assembled. The music CD is compiled in a chronologically distinct and meaningful fashion. The music coincides with a schedule based on the calendar of Christian feast days, beginning with the Feast of the Annunciation commemorated in March, and leading up to and including those of the Advent season, Christmas, and post-Christmas Day. The music program is essentially constructed on the schedule and organization of the Mass, a decision easily rendered since a number of works for *Sacred Christmas Music* were composed for specific parts of the Mass. They include compositions for Midnight Mass and the Feast of the Holy Innocents (December 28). Superimposed on this schedule are sacred pieces for church-prescribed prayer services, known as the "canonical hours," that were mandated for Christmas Day and were part of the Divine Office. Important additions to this sacred lineup are Gregorian chant as well as two of our much-loved carols. The sequence of the music CD is listed as follows (note that titles appearing in all capital letters indicate official parts of the Mass):

Music Title:	Church Feast Day
Hört zu ihr lieben Leute	March 25—The Annunciation
Veni, Emmanuel	December 17–23
Jesu, Joy of Man's Desiring	Fourth Sunday of Advent and July 2
(*Jesu, bleibet mein freude*)	Feast of the Visitation to the
	Virgin Mary

Concerto Grosso in G Minor, Op.6/8	Christmas
O magnum mysterium	Christmas
KYRIE	Christmas Third Mass
GLORIA	Christmas / all High Masses
GRADUAL: *Tecum principium*	Christmas Midnight Mass
Messiah: For unto Us a Child Is Born	Christmas and Easter
ALLELUIA: *Dominus dixit*	Christmas Midnight Mass
OFFERTORY: *Anima nostra*	December 28—The Holy Innocents
Panis angelicus	Some High Masses
Messiah: Hallelujah Chorus	Advent and Easter
The Lord's Prayer	All Masses
Hodie Christus natus est	Vespers—late afternoon or early evening Christmas
Silent Night (Stille nacht, heilige nacht)	Christmas

Imagine attending the Mass or meditating on the Divine Office seven or eight hundred years ago! Even though much of the program's music was composed centuries later by composers whose quality of work is recognized and appreciated throughout the Christian and Western worlds, imagine the celebration of Christmas with church services and prayer . . . and soaring sacred music!

The music program softly begins with *Hört zu ihr lieben Leute,* a beautiful German motet arranged by Michael Praetorius, a noted Lutheran music scholar and one of the most prolific composers of church music of his age. His sacred adaptation engenders respect for the creative work of the lyric composer who set out to commemorate the Feast of the Annunciation, the precedent of the Nativity itself.

Veni, Emmanuel, a carol with an intriguing history and wholly sacred tone, is a Latin hymn of seven verses reputedly composed by monastery monks for the seven nights preceding the vigil of Christmas (Christmas Eve), from December 17 through December 23. It was later discovered to have originated as a funeral processional chant and was adapted to the Advent text by a nineteenth-century English clergyman. The exhilarating profusion of organ, carillon, bell ringing, and brass instruments creates a stirring effect, making this one of the more memorable instrumental versions of *Veni, Emmanuel.*

Imagine meditating then before worship services begin and hearing the soothing sounds of Johann Sebastian Bach and his "Jesu, Joy of Man's Desiring" *(Jesu, bleibet mein freude),* a cantata the great composer had originally dedicated for the fourth Sunday of Advent before revising it for a July church feast day.

Imagine, too, then being feted by the glorious sounds of the *Concerto Grosso in G Minor, Op.6/8* (or "Christmas Concerto") by Arcangelo Corelli, one of Italy's more renowned Baroque composers. His music soars triumphantly and fluidly through its various movements. Such was the power of that concerto, in fact, and of other beautiful Italian Baroque concerti, that I launched my efforts to answer the question: "When did Christmas music begin?" The discovery of this special Christmas music opened the floodgates to the wonders of the Baroque era, as well as to sacred

Singing Angels
1432 left panel from
Ghent Altarpiece
Jan Van Eyck (c. 1390–1441) &
Hubert Van Eyck (c.1370–1426),
Netherlandish
St. Bavo Cathedral,
Ghent, Belgium

polyphony, and propelled me on a quest to trace the development of Christmas music from the early centuries of Christianity to the twenty-first century.

The glory of polyphony continues with *O magnum mysterium*, a motet based on an ancient Latin responsory prayer. Tomás Luis de Victoria's mystic composition, like other motets sung for devotional services outside the Mass, reveals the religious soul of Spain and captures the solemnity of shepherds witnessing an unusually humble scene in Bethlehem. More ancient music follows. First is the "Kyrie" from Giovanni Luigi Palestrina's *Missa: Hodie Christus natus est*, an ornate polyphonic setting that arrives as though inspired by pious incantations of Greek scribes pouring over ancient sacred texts. You can almost sense God Almighty nodding his approval in the background. And then follows the "Gloria," an early second century Christian prayer set to music by Joaquin Desprez. His creative genius and versatility as a composer of sacred music accentuates the angels' memorable proclamation: *"Gloria in excelsis Deo et in terra pax hominibus bonae voluntatis"* (Glory to God in the highest and on earth peace to men of good will), the most recited phrase regarding the good news of Christ's birth.

The "Gradual: *Tecum principium*," a Gregorian chant for Midnight Mass, sheds

The Midnight Mass
1911 oil on canvas
Edward Timothy Hurley
(1869–1950), American
Cincinnati Art Museum

light on the monophonic range of ancient church music. It is a forbear of music that is to come in the second millennium. Two excerpts from Handel's *Messiah,* considered one of the greatest pieces of music the Western world has ever known, reaffirms the majesty of sacred music. "For unto Us a Child Is Born" and the "Hallelujah Chorus" not only illustrate Handel's musical genius, but they also bear witness to the beauty that can be achieved when talent is infused with mighty inspiration. Such magnificence adroitly serves as bookends for the plainchant "Alleluia: *Dominus dixi,*" the classical pieces of *Anima nostra,* and *Panis angelicus.*

Anima nostra, an Offertory prayer commemorating the Feast of the Holy Innocents—part of the biblical sequence after the birth of Christ—as it is sung by the world-renowned Vienna Boys Choir clearly demonstrates the beauty of Latin phrasing. *Panis angelicus,* a time-honored prayer written by the great theologian, St. Thomas Aquinas, continues the inspiring string of Latin classics. Initially conceived for the Benedictus, the thirteenth-century prayer has also been associated with the rites of Communion. The music of César Franck, an eminent nineteenth-century French composer and organist, superbly complements the majesty of St. Aquinas's words.

What follows is the reverential setting of "The Lord's Prayer" (Our Father) by Albert Hay Malotte, a little-known American composer whose fame shall ever be associated with his remarkable score for one of the Bible's oldest prayers. Known as the *Pater noster* in the Latin Mass, "The Lord's Prayer" reaches ethereal heights with the performance of the Mormon Tabernacle Choir and Philadelphia Orchestra.

Concluding the Latin entries of the music program is *Hodie Christus natus est,* a motet based on the liturgy of Vespers for Christmas Day. (Vespers is another of the "canonical hours" of prescribed daily prayers recited in the late afternoon or early evening.) Here again the listener is exalted by the rich legacy of sixteenth-century polyphony. The music of Jan Pieterszoon Sweelinck captures the heart and soul of the common man and reaffirms the good news of the angels: the Lord and Savior Jesus Christ has been born in the city of David, known as Bethlehem.

Last, as the night beckons us to take leave of Midnight Mass, or Christmas Eve service, when we are still warmed by the good tidings of the Gospel and the fellowship of neighbors and parishioners, imagine wending home with family, the soul still aglow from sharing a wondrous celebration of faith and religious affirmation. Imagine, too, the night air is crisp, and cold, as you gaze at the heaven's treasury of luminous stars, searching for that one special brilliant light. Imagine the stillness, pervasive in time and space and seamless. And imagine from out of the deep clear blue a faint sound wafts through the distance, the heart intuitively responding to the quiet broken by the gentle striking of carillon bells.

And slowly those bells amplify from barely perceptible notes to soft angelic strains. Slowly they toll reverential, humble notes as though summoning to the manger poor shepherds in awe of God's angels. And before long as they toll with sweet praise in commemoration of that special moment two thousand years ago, the last strain of "Silent Night" tolls of peace on earth and covers all.

Alleluia

c. 1885 tapestry
designed by Edward Burne-Jones
(1833–1898), English
Harris Museum and Art Gallery,
Lancashire, UK

Music Collection

1 Anima nostra

ENGLISH TITLE:
Our Soul

RECORDING ARTISTS:
*The Vienna Boys Choir,
Hans Gillesberger, conductor*

WORDS:
Biblical text from Psalms

MUSIC:
*Michael Haydn
(1737–1806),
Austrian composer*

"ANIMA NOSTRA," POSSESSING THE CLASSICAL vocal sound of a type of church music advanced by Viennese composers, comes from Psalm123, verse 4. It was composed as an Offertory prayer since it was customary for psalms to form the core of the textual repertory of the Mass Propers, which includes the Offertory (in which the bread and wine are presented, or offered, to God before they are consecrated), as well as the Divine Office. This practice was inherited from ancient Jewish services and eventually became part of Church tradition. Originally the Mass Propers was sung in primitive chant before being replaced by the more ornate Roman chant.

The Offertory is one of five parts of the Mass Propers; the other four include the Introit, Gradual, Alleluia, and Communion, all of which became a standard feature of the Church by 600 A.D. although the Psalm selection would vary from Mass to Mass.

Michael Haydn, the younger brother of Joseph Haydn (1732–1809), one of Austria's most famous composers, wrote the music of *Anima nostra* in 1787. Michael was a master in his own right, having composed over four hundred pieces of religious music during his lifetime. His career began as a chorister in Vienna, included his appointment to the court of the Bishop of Grosswardein, now part of northern Romania, and later appointment as Konzertmeister to the Archbishop of Salzburg. He was also skilled at the organ and taught the violin.

Michael Haydn's devout works included sixty-five Offertory settings, among which was *Anima nostra* composed for the Offertory for the Holy Innocents *(Offertorium pro festo ss. Innocentium)* to honor the infants who were slaughtered by Herod's soldiers, a tragic event cited in the New Testament Gospel of St. Matthew 3:16-18:

Then Herod, when he saw that he was mocked of the wise men, was exceedingly wroth, and sent forth, and slew all the children that were in Bethlehem, and in all coasts thereof, from two years old and under, according to the time which he had diligently inquired of the wise men. Then was fulfilled that which was spoken by Jeremy the prophet, saying, In Rama was there a voice heard, lamentation, and weeping, and great mourning, Rachel weeping for her children, and would not be comforted, because they are not.

According to the Nativity narrative, the fearful Herod wanted to kill the new-born Christ Child, hoping to accomplish his sinister plan by slaying all the infants from Bethlehem and adjoining areas that were two years old or younger. December 28 was thus set aside by the Church as the feast day to commemorate this wanton slaughter of so many innocent children.

LATIN

Anima nostra
sic ut passer,
erepta est de laquea venantium:
laqueus contritus est,
et nos liberati sumus.

ENGLISH

Our soul
is exceedingly filled
with the scorning of those
that are at ease,
and with the contempt of the proud.

The Massacre of the
Innocents
c. 1565 oil on panel,
Pieter Bruegel, the Elder
(1525–1569), Flemish
Kunsthistorisches Museum,
Vienna

2 Concerto Grosso in G Minor, Op. 6/8

ENGLISH TITLE:
*Christmas Concerto;
Pastoral for the
Holy Nativity*

ITALIAN TITLE:
*Pastorale per il
Santissimo Natale*

RECORDING ARTISTS:
*Kammerorchester Carl Philipp
Emanuel Bach (Carl Philipp
Emanuel Bach Chamber
Orchestra); Hartmut
Haenchen, conductor*

MUSIC:
*Arcangelo Corelli, Italian
(1653–1713),
Baroque composer and
violinist*

DURING THE SEVENTEENTH and eighteenth centuries, the evolution from strictly vocal to an instrumental style was well advanced. An instrument vital to this changeover in Italy was the violin, which was replacing the viola da gamba in importance. It is understandable why some of Italy's top composers were also violinists. This was also the era when the music world became indebted to Andrea Amati (1525–1611) of Cremona and Antonius Stradivarius (1644–1737), both Italians and superb craftsmen famed for their creation of superior violins.

An important figure in this changeover was Arcangelo Corelli, a noted violinist and composer who had considerable influence on large ensemble musical productions. One of these productions was his *Concerto Grosso in G Minor, Op.6/8,* better known as "Christmas Concerto," that was part of a series of twelve similar works.

Collectively known as *Concerti Grossi Op. 6,* this remarkable series was not published until after Corelli's death at the Italian master's request. Perhaps Corelli was imitating a standard set four years earlier by Guiseppe Torelli (1658–1709), another eminent violinist and Italian musician whose own Christmas Concerto was published posthumously. More likely, Corelli's request was borne of his unpretentious nature, one engendered by an easy-going disposition and personal humility.

Corelli, who spent almost his entire life in Rome, gained an international reputation solely for his contributions to instrumental music, which is the only type of music he composed. Musicians from Europe and England admired him for his novel compositions, and his *Concerti Grossi Op. 6* was particularly popular because of its wonderful balance and brilliance. Eleven years after his death, a group of musicians from the London Academy were so inspired by his masterpiece that they reputedly played all twelve works of the Concerti Grossi at a single sitting!

The influence of Corelli was so great that it extended to the following generation of composers, one dominated by Johann Sebastian Bach and George Frederic Handel, the giants of the Baroque era. Handel was so captivated by the works of Corelli that in 1707 he briefly worked with the Italian composer during a special visit to Rome, where Corelli had spent most of his life. Corelli's influence also extended to royal and church circles, from whose patrons he gained considerable support for his musical talent.

The concerto form developed by Corelli reflected some of the finest aspects of the Baroque style, one characterized by strong, flowing, expressive dissonant features; a largeness of scale; and massiveness of proportion. The concerto was usually a single instrument, or a small group of instruments, pitted against a whole orchestra. This affluence of musical sound would become very popular during his time, as it still is today, by lovers of that musical genre.

Concerto Grosso in G Minor, Op.6/8 is the most famous of many Christmas Concertos. Besides those created by Corelli and Torelli, Francesco Manfredini (1680–1748), a noted choirmaster at the cathedral of Pistoia, and other composers produced similarly titled works. By and large these concertos included a pastoral movement setting to be played in church on the night before Christmas. The front page of the Christmas Concerto conceived by Corelli is clearly inscribed with the words *fatto per la notte di Natale,* meaning "made for Christmas Night."

The origin of the Christmas Concerto is attributed to an Italian folk custom. Peasants and shepherds from the surrounding countryside would venture into the nearby towns to re-enact the Nativity scene of the shepherd's adoration of the Christ Child, a practice inherited from medieval liturgical drama, during a Novena, a nine-day devotional period of the Catholic Church just preceding Christmas Day. The re-enactment was accompanied by music performed by twosomes, one playing melody on the shawm, a wind instrument and forerunner of the oboe, and the other playing on the bagpipes.

From such humble beginnings, the pastoral color and character of the Italian concerto, especially as provided by Corelli and his "Christmas Concerto," brings a regal quality to the musical celebration of the birth of Jesus Christ.

3 Gloria

MANY COMPOSERS since the embryonic stage of polyphony have written their own original music for the Roman Mass. Josquin Desprez, acknowledged as the greatest composer of the High Renaissance and one of the most influential composers in the history of Western music, was no different in that respect, except that he took it to heights unknown in his time.

A master of the sixteenth-century style of polyphonic vocal music, Josquin (pronounced Jas-can) was compared to Michelangelo in terms of greatness by Cosimo Bartoli (1503–1575), an Italian humanist and philosogist, in his *Ragionamenti academici* (Venice, 1567). Josquin's superior abilities as a composer also found an admirer in Martin Luther, the leader of the Reformation who was known to be effusive in his praise of Josquin as the "master of the notes."

Like most great artists, there was an individualistic streak to Josquin, as he pretty much composed as he pleased. However, he conveyed the meanings of the words he set in such an extraordinarily expressive and melodic way that he drew strong opposition from some of his contemporaries, who were wedded to the medieval tradition of more abstract music. This new musical direction, representing the highest achievement of his time, matured over a two-decade period when Josquin served in several court chapels, notably that of Cardinal Ascanio Sforza, and as a member of the papal choir. In 1501 he left the papal choir and went to France to serve in Louis XII's court as *maestro di cappella*, meaning "director of chapel choir," for which he was richly rewarded as the highest-paid singer in the chapel's history.

By the time of his death in 1521, Josquin had influenced many musicians who came in contact with him or his music. He wrote in all the most significant vocal forms of the High Renaissance, including Masses, where most of the compositional innovations were taking place, as well as for motets and secular pieces. His motets especially possessed a depth of feeling and piety that epitomized a uniquely expressive style that is still admired today.

Josquin's version of the "Gloria" is truly a glorious piece that demonstrates his gift for melody and brings genuine beauty to the liturgical text. The text itself might go back as far as the second century. One of the most ancient examples of hymnody in the early church, it can be traced to Syrian and Greek sources. A Latin version appeared around 690 A.D., a time when the Gloria was reserved only for Christmas.

Also known as the "Greater Doxology," today the Gloria remains part of the Ordinary of the Mass, i.e., the portion of the liturgy that remains unchanged from one Mass to the next. About fifty-six melodies of the Gloria have been found in medieval manuscripts, an indicator of just how much the Church valued this very ancient prayer.

Heavenly angels supposedly sang the first two lines of this beloved prayer to poor shepherds tending their flocks of sheep on a wondrous night when Christ the Redeemer was born in Bethlehem.

Josquin Desprez
1611 woodcut after
a cathedral painting
Lebrecht Music & Art Collection,
London

The Nativity from The Sforza Hours
1490 Flemish illuminated manuscript
British Library, London

LATIN

Gloria in excelsis Deo
Et in terra pax hominibus bonae volutatis.
Benedicimus te, glorificamus te.
Gratias agimus tibi propter magnum
gloriam tuam.
Domine Deus, rex coelestis,
Deus Pater omnipotens,
Domine Fili unigenite Jesu Christe,
Domine Deus, Agnus Dei,
Filius Patris,
Qui tollis peccata mundi,
Miserere nobis,
Suscipe deprecationem nostram,
Qui sedes ad dexteram Patris,
Miserere nobis.
Quoniam tu solus sanctus,
Tu solus Dominus,
Tu solus Altissimus, Jesu Christe,
Cum Sancto Spiritu in Gloria
Dei Patris, Amen.

ENGLISH

Glory to God in the highest
And on earth peace to men of good will.
We bless thee, we glorify thee.
We give thanks to thee for thy
great glory.
Lord God, King of heaven,
God the Father omnipotent,
Lord, the only-born Son, Jesus Christ,
Lord God, Lamb of God,
Son of the Father,
Who taketh away the sins of the world,
Have mercy on us.
Accept our entreaties,
Who sitteth at the right hand of the Father,
Have mercy on us.
For thou alone art holy.
Thou alone Lord,
Thou alone the most high, Jesus Christ,
With the Holy Spirit in the glory
of God the Father. Amen.

4 Gregorian Chant

RECORDING ARTISTS:
The Trappist Monks of the Abbey of Gethsemani

WORDS:
Ancient church liturgy from the third to sixth centuries and biblical texts

MUSIC:
Ancient church compositions from the ninth to thirteenth centuries

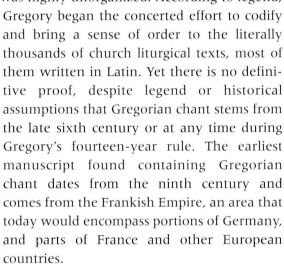

SELECTIONS
(FROM CHRISTMAS MASSES):
1. GRADUAL: *Tecum principium* (MODE II)
2. ALLELUIA: *Dominus dixit* (MODE VIII)

Gregorian chant, i.e., Western chant or plainchant, as musicologists prefer to call it, was named after Pope Gregory I (540–604 A.D.), also known as Gregory the Great. Born of a wealthy patrician family, Gregory followed a career in public life that left him personally dissatisfied, eventually leaving it to begin a life of piety and contemplation. At the age of thirty-four he became a Benedictine monk, built seven monasteries with his own money, and was the first monk to be elected pope in 590 A.D.

His monastic life had brought him close to church music, providing him with the knowledge that church music was highly unorganized. According to legend, Gregory began the concerted effort to codify and bring a sense of order to the literally thousands of church liturgical texts, most of them written in Latin. Yet there is no definitive proof, despite legend or historical assumptions that Gregorian chant stems from the late sixth century or at any time during Gregory's fourteen-year rule. The earliest manuscript found containing Gregorian chant dates from the ninth century and comes from the Frankish Empire, an area that today would encompass portions of Germany, and parts of France and other European countries.

What is not subject to question is Gregory's desire to bring order and conformity to Church liturgy from the vast stores of sacred texts. His strong interest in music was supposedly demonstrated by his active collection of a rather large repertory of Roman chants, which may have numbered three thousand pieces at the time, and at his papal behest Roman chant would eventually spread throughout the continent and supersede all other chants in usage. Also, at his behest, monastic groups were formed to serve basilicas, the ancient churches of Rome accorded special ceremonial rites by the pope. These groups formulated chant based on verses from Psalms of the Old Testament, but there is no musical evidence to verify these chants as being Gregorian. One reason for this lack of evidence was that notation was still unknown.

One of the most important developments in the history of Western music, influenced by the ancient Greeks, who had practiced naming different music pitches with letters a thousand years earlier, notation evolved as a mnemonic device for singers who were already familiar with melody and words.

Encouraged by the Christian Church and arising from plainchant of the Middle Ages, this device, which at first did not denote pitch, eventually enabled composers of liturgical texts, who were mostly monks, to begin placing primitive signs called "neumes" over manuscript texts to represent in which direction a melody should go: up or down. However, these early and more primitive musical signs, surviving today in transcriptions of Gregorian chant, did not denote duration.

Notation quickly enhanced the growth of Gregorian chant, which by the eighth century was in competition with, or descended from, other chants from the ancient Church, including Ambrosian, from the early Christian Church and named after St. Ambrose, the bishop of Milan; Mozarabic, from Spanish rites; Gallican, from ancient Gaul (France); Byzantine, from the Eastern Church; and Old Roman, from the earliest days of empire. There were other chants, of course, that existed then, as they have throughout all history, which served the impulses of primitive sects besides the more established religions of Eastern and Western societies.

The origins of Christian liturgical chant for both Eastern and Western

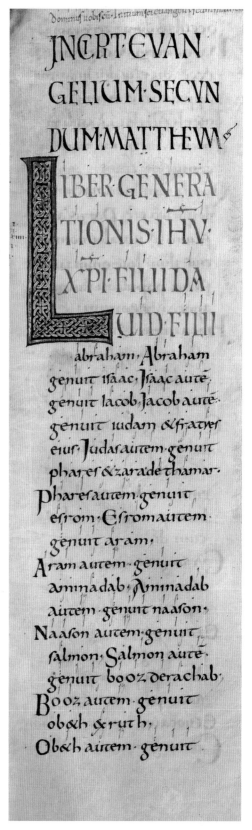

Latin rites can indeed be traced to pagan music at such early church centers as Antioch, Jerusalem, Rome, and Constantinople, besides being derived from Jewish synagogue practices. Each of these plainchant families could be distinguished by its own idiomatic modes, which for some of the repertoires of both Eastern and Western rites were assigned numbers or names. Modes were music made from notes drawn from a series of sequences, each with its own scale or fixed set of pitch intervals, a way of melodic behavior. The simplest way to remember modes is to think of them as altered major and minor scales. In the late eighth century, the repertory of Gregorian chant had assimilated the symmetrical arrangements of eight modes from Byzantine liturgical chant (four additional modes would be added during the Renaissance), and from then forward Gregorian chant listed its melodies by modes as follows:

> Dorian   (Mode I)
> Hypodorian   (Mode II)
> Phrygian   (Mode III)
> Hypophrygian   (Mode IV)
> Lydian   (Mode V)
> Hypolydian   (Mode VI)
> Mixolydian   (Mode VII)
> Hypomixolydian (Mode VIII)

The ninth century also witnessed the appearance of neumes that provided for a more exact measurement of pitch. It was also an age when Gregorian chant was maturing as a distinct entity largely as a result of the supersession and acceptance of Roman chant by Charlemagne and the Holy Roman Empire.

With the introduction of the musical staff and other notational devices during the 900–1050 period, it was possible to notate the relative pitch. By the twelfth and thirteenth centuries, Gregorian chant was a thoroughly entrenched part of church liturgy throughout all Christian Europe. It was also during this time span when Gregorian chant enjoyed its greatest prestige.

There are two critical points about Gregorian chant worth noting:
1. it was sung unaccompanied by any musical instrument;
2. it was an integral aspect of High Mass (or Solemn Mass), and other designated Church ceremonies or services, particularly the Divine Office.

The Divine Office, whose texts are also contained in the Breviary (a collection of prayers and hymns for the canonical hours), was not a sacramental service like the Mass. It was a set of prescribed prayers in honor and praise of Christ and the saints, consisting mostly of Antiphons, Psalms, and Canticles, established by the Church to be recited or sung each day by the clergy at precise times known as "the canonical hours." A term borrowed from the custom of the Jews, emulated by the Apostles, and later adopted by the early Christians, the canonical hours had a schedule of eight prayer sessions during the Middle Ages, but has since been changed and reduced to seven hours by the Vatican II Council of the 1960s.

The ancient schedule of canonical hours ensues:

2 a.m. – Matins (also known as Nocturnes and Vigils)
5 a.m. – Lauds (or "Morning Prayer") just before dawn
6 a.m. – Prime (just after Lauds)
9 a.m. – Terce (3rd hour of the day)
Noon – Sext (6th hour of the day)
3 p.m. – None (9th hour of the day)
6 p.m. – Vespers (or "Evening Prayer" after sunset)
7 p.m. – Compline (or "Night Prayer" before bed)

For purposes of distinction, the *Book of Hours* was an abbreviated prayer book designed for the personal devotions of the laity. Pre-eminent libraries and museums around the world now conserve a great number of these prayer books, one of the most famous of which is *Les Très Riches Heures du Duc du Berry*. These personal prayer books were arranged according to the eight canonical hours, thus the title *Book of Hours,* and they generally consisted of the Hours of the Virgin, Gospel passages, Psalms, the Office of the Dead, the Litany of the Saints, and a liturgical calendar.

Gregorian chant, however, could be most distinguished and florid in association with the High Mass, where it was sung by the Mass celebrant, or priest. At Low Mass, all liturgy was read.

For the medieval Church, the Mass was a communion service, or Eucharist, the most important and solemn sacrament believed to have been instituted by Jesus at the Last Supper. The practice of consecrating and consuming bread and wine as the body and blood of Christ was typically celebrated by a priest at the altar. The Mass, the central practice of church liturgy and worship, consisted of two distinct sections:

1. Ordinary of the Mass: the Mass liturgy not based on biblical texts that are constant from one service to the next and will always use the same text, including the following:

KYRIE
GLORIA
CREDO (Nicene Creed)
SANCTUS (includes Benedictus)
AGNUS DEI

2. Proper of the Mass: Mass liturgy based on biblical texts, most of them Psalms, that are different for each feast day of saints, seasons of the church year, and other designated celebrations:

INTROIT
GRADUAL (or TRACT during penitential seasons, e.g., Lent)
ALLELUIA
SEQUENCE
OFFERTORY
COMMUNION

The service book of the Mass was the missal and its musical counterpart the Gradual. Although Mass settings could be polyphonic, those used here are in plainchant (Gregorian) for the liturgy of the Eucharist.

Mass is a term most often associated with the Mass of the Roman Catholic Church. The Mass was noted for the usage of Latin texts from about the fourth century until 1966, when the use of the vernacular tongue was mandated. The Anglican (Episcopal) Mass consists of the same elements, but it is usually sung in English from the *Book of Common Prayer*. Two parts of the Roman Ordinary of the Mass, the Kyrie and Gloria, are used in the Lutheran Mass.

The Gregorian chants chosen for Sacred Christmas Music are those from two Christmastide Masses. They represent the fine art of an ancient, elaborate, and beautiful monophonic style of the Latin melodies of Christmas.

1. Gradual: *Tecum principium* (Mode II) for Midnight Mass

The Gradual is an important element of the Proper of the Mass. The text for *Tecum Principium* comes from Psalm 109 or Psalm 110 depending on the Bible used. In the Latin Vulgate Bible, the text source would be Psalm 109:3 & 1, and from the Hebrew Bible it would be Psalm 110:3 & 1. Specifically incorporated as part of Christmas Midnight Mass, *Tecum principium* demonstrates to what magnificent heights Gregorian chant could soar. With the succeeding "Alleluia," it is derived from the most ancient and beautiful of the primitive Gregorian chant melodies.

Generally sung after the Epistle or the first Scripture reading, the Gradual is a responsory chant, much like that practiced at a Jewish synagogue service when a psalm or a canticle was sung by the cantor following the Readings. However, in the early Church, and in later centuries, the Gradual acted as a commentary on the scriptural reading.

It was difficult to sight-read the Gradual, and for that reason it was usually sung by highly trained singers (cantors). By the ninth and tenth centuries, Graduals were compiled in large collections called *Graduales*. Until the fourteenth century, they were frequently sung with *organum*, i.e., adding two or more voice parts to be sung simultaneously with the chant. This sophisticated musical development was encouraged by two of the most noted composers of medieval France: Leonin (or Master Leonius, active c.1163–1190) and Pérotin (or Master Perotinus, active c.1200) of Notre Dame in Paris.

Gradual from a Christmas Mass
mid 12th century manuscript page from St. Alban's Abbey
British Library, London

LATIN

Psalm 109 (110):3

Tecum principium
in die virtutis tuae:

in splendoribus sanctorum, ex utero
ante luciferum
genui te.

Psalms 109 (110):1

Dixit Dominus Domino meo:
Sede a dextris meis:
donec ponam inimicos tuos,
scabellum pedum tuorum.

ENGLISH

Psalm 109 (110):3

Thine is princely power in
     the day of Thy birth,

in holy splendor;
before the morning star.
I have begotten thee.

Psalms 109 (110):1

The Lord said unto My Lord:
"Sit thou at My right hand,
until I make Thine enemies
Thy footstool."

The Celebration of Christmas Mass at the Sainte Chapelle, Paris
early 15th century illumination from Les Très Riches Heures du Duc du Berry Limbourg Brothers (active c. 1400–1416), Flemish Musée Condé, Chantilly, France

The Virgin and Child with Angels

c. 1445 tempera on panel
follower of Fra Angelico
(c. 1387–1455),
Italian (Florentine)
National Gallery of Art, London

II. Alleluia: *Dominus dixit* (Mode VIII) for Midnight Mass

Part of the Proper of the Mass, the Alleluia and its verses were sung just before the Gospel. Alleluia chants are generally quite exuberant, as is "Alleluia: *Dominus dixit*" for the Midnight Mass of Christmas. *Alleluia* is a Hebrew word essentially meaning, "praise to God." Since the primitive and ancient Church, it has maintained its Hebrew identity. Because of its exultant character, the Alleluia is never used for requiems (Dead Masses), or from Septuagesima Sunday (the seventh Sunday before Easter) to the Vigil of Easter, a penitential time when it is replaced by the Tract.

The highly melodic "Alleluia" was probably made an official part of the Mass by Pope Damascus (368–384 A.D.). For a time it was restricted to Easter until Pope Gregory the Great extended its usage for the entire liturgical year except for the penitential periods already noted. The Alleluia generally comprises the word itself and is framed by a verse from Psalms or original poetic phrases or a combination thereof.

LATIN	ENGLISH
Alleluia, Alleluia:	Alleluia, Alleluia.

Psalm 2:7	**Psalm 2:7**
Dominus dixit ad me:	The Lord said unto me:
Filius meus es tu,	Thou art my Son,
Ego hodie genui te.	This day I have begotten Thee.
Alleluia.	Alleluia.

5 Hodie Christus natus est

ENGLISH TITLES:
Today Jesus Christ Is Born;
A Child Is Born

RECORDING ARTIST:
The Cathedral Choir of St.
John the Divine, Richard
Westenburg, conductor

WORDS:
Macaronic text from ancient
church chant from the sixth
through ninth century

MUSIC:
Jan Pieterszoon Sweelinck
(1562–1621),
Dutch composer

THE MACARONIC TEXT (containing a mixture of Latin and vernacular words) of *Hodie Christus natus est,* which is sung as chant every Christmas in the Sistine Chapel, is based on an antiphon for the *Magnificat* at Vespers, a part of the liturgy of Christmas Day. Vespers was one of the daily prayers, or canonical hours, scheduled for members of the clergy for the late afternoon or early evening. One source for the text came from the Gospel of Luke 2:11,13-14:

> *For unto you is born this day in the city of David a Saviour, which is Christ the Lord . . . And suddenly there was with the angel a multitude of the heavenly host praising God, and saying, Glory to God in the highest and on earth peace, good will toward men*

Another source for the text comes from Psalm 32:11, which reads as follows:

> *Be glad in the Lord, and rejoice, ye righteous and shout for joy, all ye that are upright in heart.*

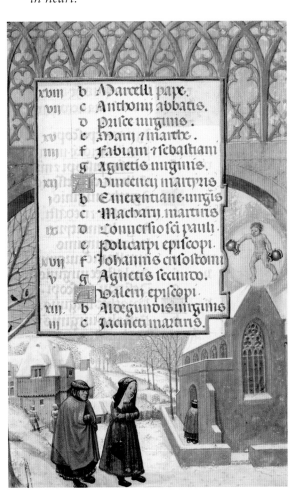

Prosperous Couple on Way to Church
Late 15th century Flemish manuscript illustration Bayerische Staatabibliothek, Munich

During his lifetime, Jan Pieterszoon Sweelinck, along with French and Flemish composers, continued to aid the extraordinary advancement of polyphony that had been made during the late Renaissance and the Reformation. That advancement was also highly supported by the nobility, or the wealthy class, primarily in the realm of secular music. Yet there was still considerable support for music that had spiritual moorings, especially that with new color and ornamentation as was the case for Sweelinck's splendid setting for the inspiring Latin-vernacular lyrics of *Hodie Christus natus est,* published in *Cantiones sacrae,* Antwerp (1619).

The music of this Dutch master, a highly respected composer who straddled the Renaissance and the Baroque eras of music, integrates traditional carol exuberance with polyphonic artistry, producing a glorious sound effect. The lively Alleluias, and the flowing, graceful Glorias, cascading like Christmas bells pealing the angels' glad tidings, further energize the exultant message of the birth of Jesus Christ.

LATIN	ENGLISH
Hodie, Hodie,	Today, today,
Christus natus est.	Jesus Christ is born!
Noe, Noe, Noe, Noe, Noe, Noe.	Noël, Noël, Noël, Noël, Noël, Noël.
Hodie, Hodie,	Today, today,
salvator apparuit,	Our Lord Savior appears.
Alleluia, Alleluia, Alleluia, Alleluia..	Alleluia, Alleluia, Alleluia, Alleluia.
"Hodie, Hodie,"	"Today, today,"
in terra canunt angeli.	A host of angels sing on earth
Laetantur archangeli.	And archangels rejoice.
Noe, Noe, Noe, Noe, Noe.	Noël, Noël, Noël, Noël, Noël.
Noe, Noe, Noe, Noe.	Noël, Noël, Noël, Noël.
Hodie, Hodie.	Today, today,
Exultant justi, dicentes:	The just exult and sing:
"Gloria, gloria in excelsis Deo	"Glory, glory to God in the highest.
Gloria in excelsis Deo."	Glory to God in the highest."
Alleluia, Noe, Noe, Noe,	Alleluia, Noël, Noël, Noël,
Alleluia, Noe, Noe, Noe,	Alleluia, Noël, Noël, Noël,
Alleluia, Noe, Noe, Noe,	Alleluia, Noël, Noël, Noël,
Noe, Noe, Noe, Noe!"	Noël, Noël, Noël, Noël!"

6 Hört zu ihr lieben Leute

ENGLISH TITLES:
O Hear Ye, Good People;
O All Ye Good People,
Give Ear

RECORDING ARTISTS:
Viva Voce Ensemble

WORDS:
Daniel Rumpius
(1549–c.1600),
sixteenth-century
German composer

MUSIC:
Daniel Rumpius;
harmonization provided by
Michael Praetorius
(1571–1621), German
composer and music scholar

Hört zu ihr lieben Leute, is a motet specifically written in honor of the religious Feast of the Annunciation. The lyrics, first published in 1587, are attributed to Daniel Rumpius, who most likely looked for inspiration from the following passage from the Gospel of Luke 1:28-31:

> And the angel came in unto her, and said, Hail, thou that art highly favoured, the Lord is with thee: blessed art thou among women. And when she saw him, she was troubled at his saying, and cast in her mind what manner of salutation this should be. And the angel said unto her, Fear not, Mary: for thou hast found favour with God. And, behold, thou shalt conceive in they womb, and bring forth a son, and shall call his name Jesus.

The Annunciation
c. 1470 tempera on wood panel
from the Orlier Altarpiece
Martin Schongauer
(c. 1445–1491), German
Musée d'Unterlinden,
Colmar, France

Michael Praetorius, a devout Lutheran whose family name was Schultheiss, provided the motet with a beautiful musical setting. A prolific composer with a keen eye toward sacred music, Praetorius wrote over 1,400 motets during his lifetime. He was known for sweeping and tender choral settings that were fore-runners to those of George Frederic Handel. Very popular in the German Lutheran courts of his day, Praetorius was greatly influenced by his father, who studied theology under the renowned Reformation leader Martin Luther and who was particularly fond of Luther's early compositions. In later years, it was Italian Baroque composers who provided inspiration for Praetorius's sacred output.

Although there are only four stanzas listed, the original text of *Hört zu ihr lieben Leute* had a total of eighteen verses. The lyrics were written in the macaronic prose style, with Latin phrasing predominant over German lyrics, thus indicating to some degree the continued influence of the ancient Church on sacred music composition. Ezra Harold Geer (1886–1957), an English organist and professor of music, provides the English translation. About Daniel Rumpius, the original com-poser, little is known. Nevertheless, his tender account of the Annunciation scene further enriches the repertory of German religious music.

<table>
<tr><td>

GERMAN-LATIN

Hört zu ihr lieben Leute
Ecce mundi gaudia
Gottes Gburt will ich deuten
Summa cum laetitia.
O virgo Maria,
Es plena gratia.

Es flog der Engel Gabriel,
Ecce mundi gaudia,
Gen Nazareth auf Gotts Befehl,

Summa cum laetitia.
O virgo Maria,
Es plena gratia.

Er grüsst ein Magdlein reine,
Ecce mundi gaudia,
Da er sie fand alleine,
Summa cum tristitia.
O virgo Maria,
Es plena gratia.

</td><td>

ENGLISH-LATIN

O all ye people, give ear,
Ecce mundi gaudia.
The story of God's birth to hear,
Summa cum laetitia.
O virgo Maria,
Es plena gratia.

The angel Gabriel flew down,
Ecce mundi gaudia,
At God's command, to
        Naz'reth town,
Summa cum laetitia.
O virgo Maria
Es plena gratia.

He greeted there a pure maid;
Ecce mundi gaudia,
He found her as alone she prayed,
Summa cum tristitia.
O virgo Maria,
Es plena gratia.

</td></tr>
</table>

Er sagt: "Ave Maria,
Ecce mundi gaudia,
Du sollt einen Sohn empfahn,
Summa cum laetitia."
O virgo Maria,
Es plena gratia.

He said, "Ave Maria
Ecce mundi gaudia,
Thou, thou a holy Son shalt bear,
Summa cum laetitia."
O virgo Maria,
Es plena gratia.

TRANSLATIONS (LATIN)

Ecce mundi gaudi: Behold the joy of the world
Summa cum laetitia: With great gladness
Summa cum tristitia: With great sadness
O virgo Maria: O Virgin Mary
Es plena gratia: You are full of grace
Ave Maria: Hail Mary

The Visitation
15th century German School
Musee de l'Oeuvre de Notre
Dame, Strasbourg, France

7 Jesu, bleibet mein freude

ENGLISH TITLES:
Jesu, Joy of Man's Desiring;
Jesus, Joy of Man's Desiring

RECORDING ARTIST:
The Mormon Tabernacle
Choir with the Columbia
Symphony Orchestra;
Jerold D. Ottley, conductor

WORDS:
Martin Jahn (1620–1682),
Silesian Evangelical pastor

MUSIC:
Johann Schop (1590–1664),
German composer and
instrumentalist; harmoniza-
tion by Johann Sebastian
Bach (1685–1750), German
composer and organist

THE TWO TEXTS FOR *Jesu, bleibet mein ffreude,* come from the sixth and seventeenth verses of a hymn titled "Jesu, meiner seelen wonne" by Martin Jahn (or Janus). That hymn first appeared in the 1661 publication *Frommer Christen tagliches bet-kammerlein.* The melody was taken from a 1642 hymn titled "Werde munter mein gemuete" by Johann Schop, which in later years was made familiar by the creative harmony of Johann Sebastian Bach for the chorus closing (chorale movements #6 and #10) of his Cantata No. 147. The English lyrics "Jesu, Joy of Man's Desiring" are believed to be the work of Lord Robert S. Bridges (1844–1930), a British composer named Poet Laureate in 1913, and ancestor of Prof. Richard R. Bunbury, a significant contributor to *Sacred Christmas Music.* Bridges's version is not an actual translation of the German text but rather the result of considerable poetic license, a not unusual practice in the history of carol and hymn translations.

Bach originally composed Cantata No. 147 for the fourth Sunday of Advent in 1716, when he was in Weimar, Germany. Titled "Herz und mund und tat und Leben," he rewrote it in 1723 while he was music director and cantor at St. Thomas School in Leipzig, one of the most important German musical posts and the primary reason Bach moved his family to Liepzig. He had dedicated the cantata for the Feast of the Visitation to the Virgin Mary, a liturgical day found on the Christian calendar in July, but in modern times it is more associated with Advent as immediately anticipating the birth of Jesus Christ. For inspiration, Bach took his cue from the Gospel of St. Luke 1: 39–41:

Now Mary arose in those days and went into the hill country with haste, to a city of Judah, and entered the house of Zacharias and saluted Elisabeth. And it came to pass, that, when Elisabeth heard the salutation of Mary, the babe leaped in her womb; and Elisabeth was filled with the Holy Spirit.

Bach's position at St. Thomas allowed him to devote most of his creative energy to church music, his first love. As a result, "Jesu, bleibet mein freude," along with hundreds of his other cantatas, was written not only to fulfill his contract with the church but also as a gift for "the glory of God alone" (or SDG, meaning *soli Deo gloria,* as Bach often signed his compositions). This would have been in keeping with the wishes of Martin Luther, the leader of the Reformation who loved music and encouraged singing from the congregation, since cantatas served the purpose of underlying the Gospel of the day. Cantatas, whose librettos were based on the New Testament text, were generally sung after the reading of the Gospel.

Many authorities consider Bach the greatest composer of the Baroque era, notwithstanding the opinions of devotees of George Frederic Handel, even though Bach never traveled outside his native country. His imaginative polyphony, often imbued with intense spirituality and serenity, has inspired musicians of all stripes since his passing. In the realm of sacred music, his enormous contributions to the music repertoire are replete with majestic chorales, masses, passions, and oratorios.

Today it is not unusual to hear his music, especially *Jesu, bleibet mein freude*, performed at such events as weddings, other church services, or concerts. It is perhaps more fitting, though, that Bach's wonderful cantata is gloriously reprised as part of annual Advent or Christmas music programs.

GERMAN

Wohl mir, das ich Jesum habe,
O wie feste halt ich ihn,
Dass er mir mein Herze labe,
Wenn ich krank und traurig bin.
Jesum hab ich, der mich liebet
Und sich mir zu eigen giebet.
Ach drum lass ich Jesum micht,
Wenn mir gleich mein Herze bricht.

Jesus bleibet mein Freude
meines Herzens Trost und Saft,
Jesus wehret allem Leide,
er ist meines Lebens Kraft,
meiner Augen Lust und Sonne,
meiner Seele Schatz und Wonne,
darum lass ich Jesum nicht
Aus dem Herzen und Gesicht.

ENGLISH

Jesu, joy of man's desiring,
Holy wisdom, love most bright;
Drawn by Thee, our souls aspiring
Soar to uncreated light.
Word of God, our flesh that fashioned,
With the fire of life impassioned,
Striving still to truth unknown,
Soaring, dying round Thy throne.

Through the way where hope is guiding,
Hark, what peaceful music rings;
Where the flock, in Thee confiding,
Drink of joy from deathless springs.
Theirs is beauty's fairest pleasure;
Theirs is wisdom's holiest treasure.
Thou dost ever lead Thine own
In the love of joys unknown.

right
St. Thomas Church and School, Leipzig
1723 engraving
Johann Gottfried Krügner
the Elder, German
Bach-Archiv, Leipzig

A MANUSCRIPT IN THE VATICAN RELATES that the young Palestrina sang in the streets of Rome while offering for sale the products of his parents' farm. On one such occasion he was heard singing by the choirmaster of Santa Maria Maggiore, who was so impressed by the boy's beautiful voice and pronounced musical ability that he took on the task of musically educating the talented boy. From such humble beginnings Palestrina would grow from organist and choirmaster to influential papal composer who advanced sacred polyphony at a time when the Roman Church was looking to eradicate the incursion of secular music in its liturgy and the celebration of the Mass.

He was called the "Prince of Music" for the twenty-nine motets he composed for the *Canticle of Canticles*, a sacred work that Palestrina felt was an endeavor to appreciate divine love expressed in the Canticle. His complete works are contained in thirty-three volumes, and his contributions to the realm of sacred music were

impressive. Not only did he enhance the musical reforms of the Council of Trent, an effort supported by the urgings of St. Peter Neri (1515–1595) and several popes, but he also became familiar with the spiritual nuances of church liturgy. His talents at polyphony, in keeping with the stirrings of his own soul, helped to raise the consciousness of church elders to the possibilities of the new music and how it might be effectively utilized to bring additional solemnity to the liturgy.

Part of the Ordinary of the Mass for the Third Mass of Christmas, or the *Hodie Christus natus est* Mass, the Kyrie was sung immediately after the completion of the Introit. A supplication for mercy, it was repeated as follows:

1. Kyrie eleison: three times by the Mass celebrant;
2. Christe eleison: three times by the church congregation;
3. Kyrie eleison: three times again by the Mass celebrant, usually the priest.

The first appearance of the Kyrie in the Mass was about 350 A.D. in a litany of the Antioch-Jerusalem liturgy. The text was in Greek, as it remains today, and since it is considered part of the Ordinary of the Mass, it is unchangeable. Near the end of the fifth century, Pope Gelasuis I (492–496 A.D.) inserted it into the Mass. Pope Gregory the Great added the *Christe eleison* verses. By the tenth century the Kyrie melodies had achieved a high degree of musical complexity. Many of these melodies had tropes, i.e., the additions of new melodies or texts to existing chants, or liturgical texts and phrases. In the discovery of ancient chant manuscripts, over two hundred Kyrie chant melodies have been identified. Indirect sources of the Greek text come from Psalm 6:3 and Psalm 40:5,11.

GREEK

Kyrie eleison.
Kyrie eleison.
Kyrie eleison.

Christe eleison.
Christe eleison.
Christe eleison.

Kyrie eleison.
Kyrie eleison.
Kyrie eleison.

ENGLISH

Lord have mercy.
Lord have mercy.
Lord have mercy.

Christ have mercy.
Christ have mercy.
Christ have mercy.

Lord have mercy.
Lord have mercy.
Lord have mercy.

left
Title page of Missarum liber primus
1554 music score shows Giovanni Pierluigi da Palestina presenting his Mass to Pope Julius III
British Library, London

right
The Nativity (La Notte)
c. 1525 oil on burlap
Antonio Allegri Correggio (1489–1534), Italian
Staatliche Kunstsammlungen: Gemaldegalerie Alte Meister, Dresden

9 The Lord's Prayer

LATIN TITLE:
Pater noster

ALTERNATE
ENGLISH TITLE:
Our Father

RECORDING ARTISTS:
*The Mormon Tabernacle
Choir with the Philadelphia
Orchestra, Eugene
Ormandy, conductor*

WORDS:
*Old and New Testament
texts*

MUSIC:
*Albert Hay Malotte
(1895–1964), American
composer and organist*

A NUMBER OF MUSICAL SETTINGS for this memorable prayer have been composed over the centuries. Albert Hay Malotte's setting, first heard in 1935 on a Pittsburgh radio station, created quite a popular stir, much to the embarrassment of a music publisher who had blithely tossed the music score in a wastebasket. But the publisher quickly reclaimed the score to fulfill the hundreds of requests for the sheet music of "The Lord's Prayer."

The source of the text comes from several scriptural passages. The text from Matthew 6:9-13 of the New Testament is a verbatim transcription found in the English-language King James Bible. However, the phrase "For Thine is the kingdom and the power and the glory, forever"—derived from I Chronicles 29:11-13 of the Old Testament—does not appear in the Vulgate, the Latin transcription of the early Greek Bible by St. Jerome (340–420 A.D.), a Latin scholar and philosopher. Nor does it appear in the Douay Version of the Bible, the English translation of the Vulgate. Rather, the text was added by Protestant reformers and is typically doxological, pertaining to "giving praise to God" and often added at the end of a canticle, psalm, or hymn. Another and much different source of the prayer can be found in Luke 11:2-4 of the New Testament, the text of which follows:

And he said unto them, When ye pray, say, Our Father which art in heaven, Hallowed be thy name. Thy kingdom come. Thy will be done, as in heaven, so in earth. Give us day by day our daily bread. And forgive our sins; for we also forgive every one that is indebted to us. And lead us not into temptation; but deliver us from evil.

First taught by Jesus Christ to his disciples, "The Lord's Prayer" is perhaps the most commonly uttered prayer since the inception of Christianity. It was part of early Eastern Church services when it was most likely said in Hebrew or Greek.

Hands of an Apostle
*1508 brush drawing
Albrecht Durer (1471–1528),
German
Graphische Sammlung
Albertina, Vienna*

The Eternal Father
c. 1555 oil on canvas
Paolo Veronese (1528–1588),
Italian
Hospital Tavera, Toledo, Spain

Scribes proficient in Greek introduced the prayer of the Gospel of St. Matthew. In the late sixth century, Pope Gregory the Great declared it an official part of the Latin Mass liturgy.

Albert Hay Malotte, the composer of the music, was born in Philadelphia. Years later he moved to Hollywood, where he was employed for a time by Walt Disney Studios. There he composed scores for *Silly Symphonies* and *Ferdinand the Bull*. Though Malotte also wrote music for many religious texts, his setting for "The Lord's Prayer" has brought him the most fame. Notice the reverential tone of the Mormon Tabernacle Choir and how the choral arrangement progresses as it becomes more earnest before closing with the final dramatic phrases.

LATIN

Pater noster, qui es in coelis:
sanctificetur nomen tuum:
adveniat regnum tuum:
fiat voluntas tua, sicut in coelo,
et in terra
Panem nostrum quotidianum
da nobis hodie,
et dimitte nobis debita nostra,
sicut et nos dimittimus debitoribus nostris
Et ne nos inducas in tentationem:
Sed libera nos a malo.
Amen.

ENGLISH

Our father, which art in Heaven,
Hallowed be Thy Name.
Thy kingdom come.
Thy will be done in Earth
As it is in Heaven.
Give us this day our daily bread
And forgive us our debts
As we forgive our debtors.
And lead us not into temptation,
But deliver us from evil.
For Thine is the kingdom and the
power and the glory, forever.
Amen.

RECORDING ARTISTS:
*English Baroque Soloists
with the The Monteverdi
Choir; John Eliot Gardiner,
conductor*

WORDS:
*Biblical texts selected by
Charles Jennens
(1700–1773), sometime
English poet and librettist*

MUSIC:
*George Frederic Handel
(1685-1759), German-
English composer and
conductor*

1. FOR UNTO US A CHILD IS BORN
2. HALLELUJAH CHORUS

Born in Halle, Germany, George Frederic Handel immigrated to England in 1710 to further enhance his career in music and opera. Thirty-one years later, between August 22 and September 14, 1741, the near-destitute composer wrote his *Messiah*, an oratorio based on both Old and New Testament texts. Artfully strung together by Charles Jennens, *Messiah* told the story of the life of Jesus Christ, from birth to resurrection, in an extremely compressed form.

Handel responded to Jennens's work with a great deal of enthusiasm. After beginning the arduous task of composition in a small London house, Handel, who brought the oratorio style of music to high development, worked feverishly to complete this masterpiece, hardly stopping for rest. During the writing of the "Hallelujah Chorus," he grew so ecstatic that he called in his manservant and declared to him in a tearfully joyous manner, "I did think I did see all heaven before me, and the great God Himself."

Neal's Music Hall
*Fishamble Street, Dublin
c. 1850 drawing
F. W. Fairhold (1814–1866),
English
Lebrecht Music &
Arts Photo Library, London*

Since the work was intended for Easter festivities, the first performance of it took place on April 23, 1742, at Neal's Music Hall, Fishamble Street, Dublin, Ireland, at the invitation of the city's Lord Lieutenant, who requested of Handel to perform one of his works for charity. Handel agreed and thought it appropriate to select Jennens's work for the occasion, thus beginning a practice of offering *Messiah* for charity every year thereafter. In Dublin, both the composer and the initial performance of *Messiah* were very warmly received, raising four hundred pounds and, as a result, freeing 142 men from debtors' prison.

When Handel's *Messiah* went to the London stage a year later, however, it caused outrage among some religious leaders. They felt that the Bible should not be sung as entertainment and railed against it in their sermons. It took many performances of Handel's masterpiece before it gained universal popularity. Today *Messiah* is widely acclaimed and regarded by some musicologists as one of the Western world's finest compositions.

The last performance of *Messiah* conducted by Handel himself, occurred on April 16, 1759, at the Foundling Hospital in London. Eight days later Handel died. The death of Handel and that of Johann Sebastian Bach in 1750 officially ended the Baroque music era. Handel's remains rest at Westminster Abbey, one of the most hallowed shrines in London. Ludwig van Beethoven (1770–1827), often considered the ultimate master of composition, regarded Handel as the greatest composer the world had ever known. Another great composer, Joseph Haydn, so moved on hearing the "Hallelujah Chorus," was said to have wept like a child and exclaimed, "He is the master of us all!"

Over the years Handel's masterpiece, a more extroverted vision of the story of Christ than the more metaphysical Bach passions, has traditionally been performed during the Christmas season, despite the work's emphasis on the Passion and Resurrection of Christ. The recording artists, the English Baroque Soloists and Monteverdi Choir, lead by John Eliot Gardiner, together produce an exciting and reverential performance of *Messiah*. The use of period instruments, a wonderful touch, provides a more accurate sense of how this much esteemed oratorio would have sounded in Handel's time.

George Frederic Handel
Portrait in old age with Messiah music score
1756 oil on canvas
Thomas Hudson
(1701–1779),
British National Portrait Gallery, London

1. For Unto Us a Child Is Born

"For Unto Us a Child Is Born" is one of the more familiar choruses of *Messiah*. Its emphasis is on the Nativity, and it trumpets that the newborn Child shall hold many majestic titles as promised by the biblical text from Isaiah 9:6, whose words are adopted for the oratorio text. Its Latin counterpart, "Puer nobis nascitur," was also the title of a well-known medieval carol found in the famous 1582 *Piae Cantiones* song collection. Perhaps the earliest source for "For Unto Us a Child Is Born" predates the *Moosburg Gradual* published sometime during the 1355–1360 period. The *Moosburg Gradual*, a German manuscript, actually contained "Puer nobis nascitur" and a number of other songs derived from the twelfth and thirteenth century liturgical books in the organum repertoires of Notre Dame in Paris and St. Martial.

Oratorio and Biblical Text (Isaiah 9.6)

For unto us a Child is born,
Unto us a Son is given,
And the government shall be upon his shoulder:
And His name shall be called
Wonderful, Counsellor, the Mighty God,
The Everlasting Father, the Prince of Peace.

2. Hallelujah Chorus

One of the most famous choruses ever composed, the Bible text of which is found in Revelation 19:6, 11:15, 19:16, the magnificent "Hallelujah Chorus" makes clear Handel's unmistakable faith in his Lord God truly reigning over this world. Although the primary emphasis of the oratorio is the Passion of Christ, it is more universally sung and celebrated during the Christmas season. This is not a unique development. During the medieval period, the Passion of Christ was often commemorated during the Christmas season in mystery plays and carols.

When singing the "Hallelujah Chorus," participants rise to stand, a tradition accidentally begun by King George III. According to legend, the monarch jumped to his feet when he was frightened out of a nap by the trumpets and timpani of the "Hallelujah Chorus." In deference to the standing king, the audience followed his example, thinking he was expressing enthusiasm for the music.

Oratorio and Biblical Text

Hallelujah! for the Lord God
omnipotent reigneth.
The kingdom of this world is become
the kingdom of our Lord,
and of His Christ;
And He shall reign for ever and ever.
King of Kings, and Lord of Lords
Hallelujah!

The full text of *Messiah*, comprising fifty-three parts, contained other passages from the Old Testament, including verses from the following:

1. Haggai 2:6–7
2. Malachi 3:1–3
3. Isaiah 7:14, 9:2, 35:5–6, 40:9 and 11, 50:6, 53:3–6 and 8, 60:2–3
4. Zechariah 9:9–10
5. Lamentations 1:12
6. Job 19:25–26
7. Psalms 2:1–4 and 9, 16:10, 22:7-8, 24:7–10, 68:11 and 18, 69:20.

From the New Testament, inspiration was derived from the following:
1. St. Matthew 1:23, 11:28–30
2. St. Luke 2:8-14
3. St. John 1:29
4. Romans 8:31 and 33–34, 10:15 and 18
5. I Corinthians 15:20–21 and 51–57.

Title Page
from Messiah Oratorio
1767 reprinted music manuscript
with alterations
by Geroge Frederic Handel
Library of Congress, Washington

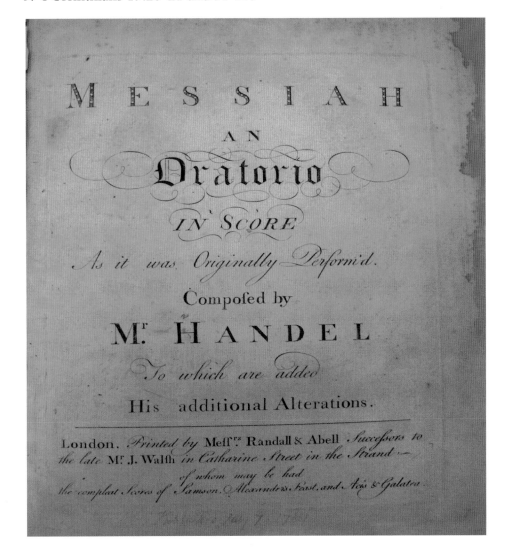

11   O magnum mysterium

ENGLISH TITLE:
O How Great the Mystery

RECORDING ARTIST:
*Westminster Cathedral
Choir; David Hill, conductor*

WORDS:
*Anonymous, ninth to twelfth
century French, or possibly
earlier*

MUSIC:
*Tomás Luis de Victoria,
a.k.a. Thomas Vittoria
(1548–1611), Spanish
priest, composer and
organist*

TOMÁS LUIS DE VICTORIA was the most significant composer of the Counter Reformation in Spain and one of the greatest composers of sacred music in the late Renaissance period. Born into a distinguished family in Avila, Spain, Victoria began his music career as a choirboy for the cathedral of Avila. When his voice changed in 1564, he was sent to the German College in Rome. He later joined a monastery founded by St. Ignatius of Loyola, where he served for a number of years as *maestro di cappella* and where in 1575 he was ordained a priest. Besides being a gifted singer, he was also a talented organist who knew and possibly studied with Giovanni Luigi Palestrina, the eminent Italian composer of Masses and motets. Victoria, considered by many to be second only to Palestrina as a composer of sacred polyphony in the sixteenth century, was so dedicated to sacred music that he never wrote any music for the secular sphere. The Spanish composer and priest probably would have known St. Teresa of Avila (1515-1582), the much honored virgin and founder of the discalced, or barefooted, Carmelite order of nuns, since they were both natives of that Spanish city.

Noted for his expressive settings of sacred Latin texts and the Mass, Victoria would often inject them with a deep sense of feeling and Spanish mysticism. Reflective of this style, but in the area of the visual arts, was the work of the artist Domenikos Theokotopoulos (1541–1614), better known as El Greco. A contemporary of Victoria, his painting *The Nativity* is imbued with the same profound sense of mysticism as Victoria's motet *O magnum mysterium.*

A fine example of high Renaissance polyphony, *O magnum mysterium* was published in 1572 as a motet for choirs of men and boys in a capella style. Victoria's setting evokes a sense of collective awe by simple shepherds attending the manger scene, one highly accentuated by a string of long free-flowing *alleluias.*

A number of talented composers of the Renaissance and later eras have created more original settings for the sacred text of *O magnum mysterium*, a Latin responsory prayer that follows the *Fourth Lesson of the Nocturn of Matins for Christmas Day.*

The Nativity
*c. 1605 oil on canvas
El Greco (1541–1614),
Greek-Spanish
Church of Charity,
Illescas, Toledo, Spain*

LATIN	ENGLISH
O magnum mysterium	O great mystery
Et admirabile sacramentum,	And how wondrous the sacrament,
Ut animalis viderent Dominum	That simple animals would behold the Lord
Natum jacentem in praesepio.	Born lying in a manger.
Beata virgo cujus viscera	Blessed be the Virgin whose womb
Meruerunt portare	Was worthy of carrying
Dominum Christum.	The Lord Christ.
Alleluia, alleluia, alleluia,	Alleluia, alleluia, alleluia,
Alleluia, alleluia, alleluia,	Alleluia, alleluia, alleluia,
Alleluia, alleluia, alleluia.	Alleluia, alleluia, alleluia.

12 Panis Angelicus

ENGLISH TITLE:
Bread of Angels

RECORDING ARTISTS:
Placido Domingo with the Vienna Boys Choir

WORDS:
St. Thomas Aquinas (1225–1274), Italian Dominican monk, philosopher, and theologian

MUSIC:
César Franck (1822–1890), Belgian-born French composer, organist, and music teacher

THE TEXT OF "PANIS ANGELICUS" COMES from the sixth stanza of *Sacris solemnis*, a venerable prayer composed as a Sequence for a Corpus Christi Mass, by Thomas Aquinas, a Dominican monk and one of the greatest theologians of the medieval age. His treatises, especially his religious tome *Summa theologica*, strongly influenced the Church's religious and philosophical direction. Most likely he used ancient Latin liturgical sources or the Scriptures as the inspiration for *Panis angelicus,* and in subsequent centuries his lyrics would be more often sung during the Benedictus of the Mass, or during Communion, since its text alludes to the act of receiving the bread of the Holy Eucharist.

Educated in the Benedictine monastery at Monte Cassino from the age of five, Thomas Aquinas later grew attracted to the Dominican Order, an aspiration seriously opposed by his family, who had him imprisoned and then contracted a prostitute to seduce him. But Thomas successfully resisted this temptation, and according to legend two angels comforted him and brought him a belt of chastity. One of the great philosophers of the Middle Ages, he taught many years at Paris University before retiring to Naples to write *Summa theologica*. During the course of writing the famous treatise, he was known to pray before the crucifix. On one occasion, another legend holds, Christ on the crucifix spoke to him.

César Franck, the composer of the music for *Panis angelicus,* was a professor at the Paris Conservatory, where he was appointed more for his ability to play the organ than as a composer. Despite this lesser status, Franck, born in Liege, Belgium, was an important figure who helped to change the direction of French instrumental music in the second half of the nineteenth century. Instrumental music had fallen out of favor in the frivolous world of the Second Empire. Under Franck's careful tutelage, his pupils at the Paris Conservatory served as the vanguard for writing original instrumental pieces, especially for the organ.

Composed in 1872 when Franck served as organist at the Church of Ste. Clotilde, *Panis angelicus* was interpolated as part of his *Mass for Three Solo Voices*, the original version of which was written in 1860. Most recordings of this ancient Latin prayer, however, generally include only one stanza of lyrics. Franck chose an organ composition to complement the words of Thomas Aquinas. Until the eighteenth and nineteenth centuries, the organ generally alternated verses with chant and polyphony. It did not usually accompany the voice. The earliest known music for the organ to have survived is the *Robertsbridge Codex*, written approximately fifty years (c. 1325) after the death of Thomas Aquinas.

The classical combination of Franck's sacred setting and Aquinas's splendid Latin prayer illuminate Christ's humanity here on earth, beginning with his birth in Bethlehem, as well as his deity, particularly his enshrinement in the Divine Trinity.

LATIN

Panis angelicus
fit panis hominum
Dat panis coelicus
figuris terminum:
O res mirabilis
manducat Dominum,
Pauper, servus, et humilis.
Te trina Deitas
unaque poscimus,
Sic nos tu visita,
sicut te colimus;
Per tuas semitas
duc nos quo tendimus,
Ad lucem quam in habitas.
Amen.

ENGLISH

The bread of angels becomes
the bread of men:
The heavenly bread brings
an end to prefigurations;
O what a wonder!
The Lord becomes the food
of the poor, the slave, the humble one.
You threefold,
single Deity,
we ask You to visit us
just as we worship You,
By Your paths lead us
where we are to go,
to the light where You dwell.
Amen.

**St. Thomas Aquinas
at Prayer**
c. 1492 illumination
from Psalter and Hours of
Alphonso V of Aragon
British Library, London

ENGLISH TITLES:
Silent Night, Holy Night;
Silent Night; Holy Night

RECORDING ARTIST:
John Klein, carillon

WORDS:
Joseph Mohr (1792–1848),
Austrian Catholic priest

MUSIC:
Franz Gruber (1787–1863),
Austrian church organist
and composer

PERHAPS THE BEST-KNOWN CHRISTMAS CAROL of all time, having been translated in hundreds of different languages and dialects, "Stille nacht, heilige nacht" (Silent Night) has an intriguing history about its origin. One account passed down over the years describes the following scene: On Christmas Eve in 1818, Franz Gruber, the church organist, had to quickly re-arrange the music after the organ of his small village church, St. Nicholas of Oberndorf, Austria, had broken down. Needing a different musical setting to go along with the poetic lyrics of the Rev. Joseph Mohr, a Catholic priest and assistant pastor, the church organist composed a melody in two hours for two solo voices, a chorus, and guitar. As a result of the creative labors of both assistant pastor and organist, the Christmas music repertoire was rewarded with what would become one of its most devotional carols.

There is considerable doubt about this account, however, and it is believed Franz Gruber had originally composed the music for guitar some time earlier. Moreover, the Rev. Mohr's six-stanza poem was written two years before, when the young priest was in the service of another parish church in Austria.

Holy Night
oil on panel triptych
Fritz von Uhde (1848–1911),
German,
Staatliche Kunstsammlungen:
Gemaldegalerie Neue Meister,
Dresden

What is open to speculation is the inspiration behind the lyrical poem. One account with a plausible ring does suggest a humble scenario, one in keeping with the simplicity surrounding the life of the Rev. Mohr.

According to this account, the Rev. Mohr was summoned to bless the house of a young woodsman whose wife had just given birth. At the behest of the anxious father, the priest quickly plodded through the snow to bring words of good cheer and blessings for the young mother and the house. This was a common practice in heavily Catholic Austria, permitted by the Catholic Ritual, which also allowed for local parish blessings for such items as meals, salt and water, baptism, and marriage. The account continues with the Rev. Mohr, although weary from the trek through the heavy snow, being suffused by the journey's pervasive and comforting silence, the snow, and the starry night. Upon his arrival at the woodsman's humble abode he found himself moved by the sight of a small, rough-hewn cradle where the baby lay and the woodchopper tending to his wife at a nearby bed of pine logs.

The priest was transfixed by the scene and overcome by a feeling of radiance and holiness about the place. It struck him that the surroundings bore a strong resemblance to how the birth of another child, the Infant Jesus, had been described 1,800 years earlier. After blessing the woodsman's family and home, the Rev. Mohr returned to his study and began reflecting on the scene he had just witnessed. While looking out across the snowy mountains and stars, he murmured to himself, "Silent Night, Holy Night." In this holy mood, he wrote the simple words of six stanzas that softly proclaimed the joy and peace of the first Christmas.

Six or seven years after its initial church performance, an organ repairman, reputedly hired to reconstruct the organ at St. Nicholas Church, found a copy of the carol at the church and received permission to take it home with him. Soon after, traveling singing groups began to sing "Stille nacht, heilige nacht" in different parts of Austria and ultimately in other regions of the world, further spreading the carol's popularity. The song would become exceptionally popular in the United States after World War I when returning war veterans remembered hearing it sung by German soldiers during a Christmas truce.

For a time the carol was thought to be either of anonymous origin or from the hand of Johann Michael Haydn (1737–1806), who was noted for his compositions of sacred music (as well as for being the brother of the more famous Joseph Haydn). The carol was probably first published in a collection of "four genuine Tyrolean songs"—songs from the Tyrol, considered part of the eastern Alps including parts of Austria and Italy—during the 1838–1842 period. When King Frederick Wilheim IV of Prussia first heard it, he was so impressed by the humble carol that he directed his court musicians to find out who composed it, a directive that may have spared "Silent Night" from obscurity. He also decreed the carol was to be sung for him every Christmas Eve, leading to another tradition that the carol should be performed every year in a special five p.m. service on Christmas Eve at St. Nicholas Church. In Austria today, the carol cannot be played in any commercial venue, or church, before five p.m. on Christmas Eve.

In ensuing years there were several English translations of "Silent Night." One of them, the widely accepted version by the Rev. John Freeman Young (1820–1885), was first published in 1859 during his tenure as assistant minister at Trinity Church in New York City in *Carols for Christmas Tide*, a publication by Daniel Dana Jr. The Rev. Young, who later served as the Episcopal bishop of Florida in 1867, was the editor of this seven-carol publication. However, he reduced and translated the original six-stanza German poem to only three and in a different sequence: verses 1, 6, and 3.

The wonderful result of these developments was a simple, loving, tender song, resonating even today with the true meaning of Christmas. Is it any surprise, then, that "Silent Night" now ranks as the most-recorded carol in history?

GERMAN	ENGLISH
Stille Nacht, heilige Nacht!	Silent night, holy night,
Alles schläft, einsam wacht	All is calm, all is bright;
Nur das traute, hochheilige Paar.	Round yon virgin mother and Child,
Holder Knab im lockigen Haar:	Holy Infant so tender and mild,
Schlaf in himmlischer Ruh!	Sleep in heavenly peace,
Schlaf in himmlischer Ruh!	Sleep in heavenly peace.
Stille Nacht, heilige Nacht!	Silent night, holy night,
Gottes Sohn, o wie lacht	Shepherds quake at the sight;
Lieb' aus deinem gottlichen Mund	Glories stream from heaven afar,
Da uns schlägt die rettende Stund:	Heavenly hosts sing *Alleluia:*
Jesus in Deiner Geburt!	Christ, the Savior, is born!
Jesus in Deiner Geburt!	Christ, the Savior, is born!
Stille Nacht, heilige Nacht!	Silent night, holy night,
Die der Welt Heil gebracht;	Son of God, Love's pure light;
Aus des Himmels goldenen Hoh'n	Radiance beams from Thy holy face,
Uns der Gnaden Fulle lasst seh'n:	With the dawn of redeeming grace,
Jesum in Menschengestalt.	Jesus, Lord, at Thy birth.
Jesum in Menschengestalt.	Jesus, Lord, at Thy birth.

Stille Nacht, heilige Nacht!
Wo sich heut' alle Macht
Vaterlicher Liebe ergoss
Und als Bruder huldvoll umschloss
   Jesus dei Volker der Welt!
   Jesus dei Volker der Welt!
Stille Nacht, heilige Nacht!

right
Cloister in the Snow
1829 oil on canvas
Karl Friedrich Lessing
(1808–1880), German
Wallraff-Richartz-Museum,
Cologne

Lange schön uns bedacht,
Als der Herr vom Grimme befreit
In der vater urgrauen Zeit
  Aller Welt Schonung verhiess.
  Aller Welt Schonung verhiess.

Stille Nacht, heilige Nacht!
Hirten erst kund gemacht,
Durch der Engel Halleluja,
Tönt es laut von fern und nah:
  Jesus der Retter ist da!
  Jesus der Retter ist da!

ALTERNATE TITLES:
Veni, Immanuel; Veni, Veni, Emmanuel

ENGLISH TITLE:
O Come, O Come, Emmanuel

RECORDING ARTISTS:
Leslie Pearson and John Paice with The London Bell Ringers

WORDS:
Anonymous ninth century, or earlier, Latin prayer

MUSIC:
Anonymous European hymn from the twelfth to thirteenth centuries, possibly fifteenth to seventeenth centuries

THE TUNE FOR "VENI, EMMANUEL" may be of fifteenth to seventeenth century ancestry, although it is reputed to be much older. In some quarters, it is believed that monastery monks composed the original hymn of seven verses for this beloved carol hymn. They sang one verse per day at Vespers, the late afternoon or early evening canonical hour of prayer, for seven straight days prior to the vigil of Christmas, or Christmas Eve. Each verse was sung before and after the canticle *Magnificat* (Mary's prayer of praise and thanksgiving from the Gospel of St. Luke 1:46–55) in conjunction with Vespers from December 17 and then continued for the next six days at the same hour until December 23.

The hymn lyrics for *Veni, Emmanuel* may have evolved over the years from Gregorian plainsongs (chant), based on several plainsong phrases of the Kyrie that were supposedly found in ancient French missals. The original words were short verses or Latin antiphons known as the famous Seven Greater Antiphons, or Great "O" Antiphons of Advent, because each of them follows the same pattern: a cry of longing, or the interjection "O" for the Messiah as he was addressed in various Old Testament texts. Each interjection was then followed by the liturgical title of Christ and a plea for his speedy "coming"—O come, Emmanuel; O come, thou rod of Jesse, etc. These Latin lyrics could date from the ninth century, or perhaps even earlier, just after the time of Pope St. Gregory the Great, when they were introduced into France.

By the twelfth or thirteenth century, according to some sources, a single hymn had been formed from five of the antiphon verses, and each verse may have included a refrain. However, there is a problem with this scenario, since the earliest known written Latin lyrics of the "O" Antiphons can only be traced back to the Appendix of *Psalteriolum cantionum Catholicarum*, a 1710 Tridentine rite prayer book, mostly comprising psalms, from Cologne, Germany.

The English version, "O Come, O Come, Emmanuel," was the creation of Rev. John Mason Neale (1818-1866), a humble, scholarly, and somewhat eccentric Anglican priest accused of Catholic proclivities who was never in his lifetime adequately appreciated by his own church. For Neale, a hymn composer and noted translator of ancient Greek and Latin religious texts, the task probably came easily since he was proficient in twenty-one different languages. His first translation of *Veni, Emmanuel* was produced in 1851 for *Medieval Hymns*, but it contained only five verses, and its English title was "Draw Nigh, Draw Nigh! Immanuel." Two years later, he wrote another one with altered text for his *Neale's Carols for Christmastide*.

Over the years other translations of *Veni, Emmanuel* were made including those by John Henry Newman (1801–1890) and Henry Sloane Coffin (1877–1954). In 1906, Thomas Alexander Lacey (1853–1931) produced an English translation of all seven verses that first appeared in *The English Hymnal* (1906), and it is this latter translation that is part of *Sacred Christmas Music.*

The Rev. Thomas Helmore (1811–1890), an Anglican priest like Neale, produced a haunting adaptation of the melody for the ancient hymn in 1856 and it was coupled with the new English title "O Come, O Come, Immanuel" in his

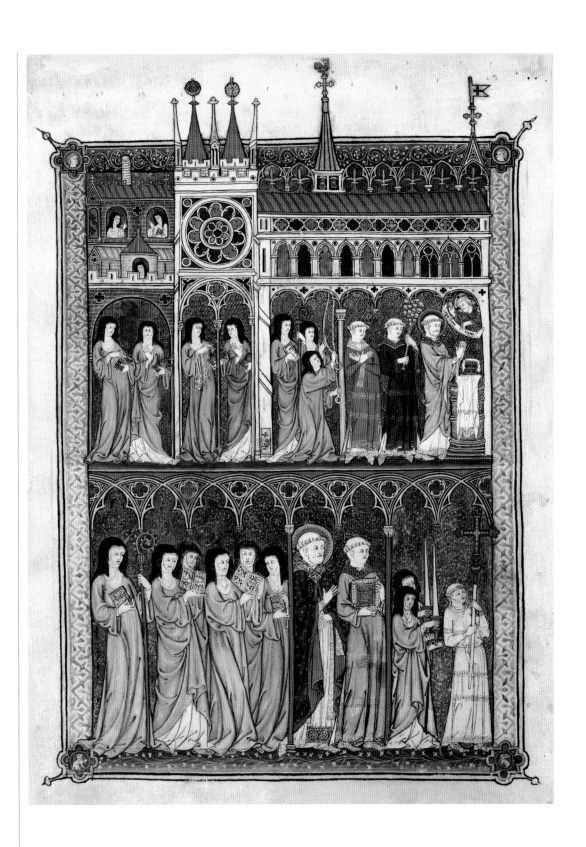

Hymnal Noted that replaced the Rev. Neale's original English translation. Because of his expertise in plainsong and Gregorian chant, Helmore was closely associated with the Rev. Neale and complemented Neale's scholarly work with ancient Greek and Latin texts. For the next twenty-two years a number of other settings were composed for *Veni, Emmanuel,* including those by Helmore, who was said to have changed some plainsongs from the twelfth and thirteenth centuries. But the oldest known tune, discovered in a French manuscript at the Bibliothèque Nationale de France in Paris, was a fifteenth-century community processional used by Franciscan nuns living in Lisbon, Portugal.

The contributions of Neale to the revitalization of ancient and medieval church hymns, especially those of Latin and Greek origin, and his deft translations of them cannot be underestimated. The brilliant scholar was known to have lamented the Reformation's neglect of the rich history of hymnody, despite the movement's praiseworthy restoration of worship and song to the language of the common people. As a result of his ceaseless efforts working with ancient hymn texts, Neale resurrected the much beloved *Veni, Emmanuel* from obscurity.

Also noteworthy about the Rev. Neale were his exemplary life and his contributions to the less fortunate. He had a penchant for caring for the lowliest on society's scale, and his Christian deeds set him apart from other clerics holding more lofty positions in the Anglican Church. Such was Neale's station in life that his own bishop, imagining Neale of Roman Catholic leanings, prohibited him from performing any ministerial duties and relegated him to a seemingly less desirable post. Thus, in 1846 Neale was made warden of Sackville College, a position he held for the rest of his life. Sackville College, however, was not a college at all! It was actually an almshouse, a charitable residence for the poor and aged. Twelve years later the humbly intrepid, and often frail and sickly, Neale founded the Sisterhood of St. Margaret, a group dedicated to the poor, needy, and suffering. For this charitable effort he was accused of a return to nuns, again earning him the enmity of Anglican Church authorities that thought he was converting to the Roman Catholic faith. Neale's ministry later established an orphanage, a school for girls, and a home for unwed mothers, but the latter was forced to close in the face of church and local opposition. In a nutshell, Neale's dedication to serving the poor and indigent was on a level with that of his work with sacred texts and hymns. Each pursuit was performed tirelessly, with dignity, and for the higher good.

Emmanuel, meaning "God with Us," is a splendid title for the carol hymn, and it must have held special significance to Rev. Neale as he worked among the poor. The title reaffirms the religious concept of Christ's birth as God Incarnate dwelling among men and announcing to them his mission here on earth. In the world of the ancient Hebrew, the choice of name was made judiciously, as the name Emmanuel must have been for Neale. For the scholarly Anglican priest, the name radiated in bold light and demonstrated, coincidentally, his own essential character and purpose as a man.

Today, *Veni, Emmanuel* is generally sung in four or fewer stanzas. It is rare to find a hymnal carrying all seven stanzas. There is no doubt that the possibly long and storied evolution of this highly devotional carol hymn, as well as its creator, an exemplary Christian role model, have provided us with a sacred and exceptional Christmas gift.

LATIN	ENGLISH
Veni, veni Emmanuel	O come, O come, Emmanuel,
Captivum solve Israel,	And ransom captive Israel
Qui gemit in exilio	That mourns in lonely exile here
Privatus Dei Filio.	Until the Son of God appear.
REFRAIN:	REFRAIN:
Gaude, gaude, Emmanuel,	Rejoice, rejoice! Emmanuel
Nascetur pro te Israel.	Shall come to thee O Israel.
Veni, O jesse virgula	O come, thou Rod of Jesse, free
Ex hostis tuos ungula,	Thine own from Satan's tyranny.
De specu tuos tartari	From depths of hell thy people save
Educ, et antro barathri.	And give them victory o'er the grave.
REFRAIN:	REFRAIN:
Veni, veni O Oriens	O come, thou dayspring, come and cheer
Solare nos adveniens,	Our spirits by thine advent here;
Noctis depelle nebulas	Disperse the gloomy shades of night
Dirasque noctis tenebras.	And death's dark shadows put to flight.
REFRAIN:	REFRAIN:
Veni Clavis davidica	O come, thou Key of David, come
Fegna reclude caelica	And open wide our heavenly home;
Fac iter tutum superum	Make safe the way that leads on high,
Et claude vias inferum.	And close the path to misery.
REFRAIN:	REFRAIN:
Veni, O Sapientia,	O come, thou Wisdom from on high,
Quae hic disponis omnia;	Who orderest all things mightily;
Veni, viam prudentiae	To us the path of knowledge show,
Ut doceas et gloriae.	And teach us in her ways to go.
REFRAIN:	REFRAIN:
Veni, veni, Adonai,	O come, O come, thou Lord of might,
Qui populo in Sinai	Who to thy tribes on Sinai's height
Legem dedisti vertice	In ancient times didst give the law,
In majestate gloriae.	In cloud, and majesty, and awe.
REFRAIN:	REFRAIN:

Veni, veni, Rex gentium
Veni, Redemptor omnium,
Ut salvas tuos famulos
Peccati sibi conscios.
                    REFRAIN:

O come, Desire of nations, bind
In one the hearts of all mankind;
Bid thou our sad divisions cease,
And be thyself our King of Peace.
                    REFRAIN:

TEXT BASED ON THE GREAT "O" ANTIPHONS OF ADVENT:

December 17:
(from Ecclesiastes 24:5)

O Sapientia quae ex ore Altissimi
prodiisti, attingens a fine usque
ad finem, fortiter suaviterque
disponens omnia: veni ad docendum
nos viam prudentiae.

O Wisdom, You came forth from the
mouth of the Most High, and reaching
from beginning to end, You ordered all
things mightily and sweetly. Come, and
teach us the way of prudence!

December 18:
(from Exodus 6:13)

O Adonai, et Dux domus Israel, qui
Moysi in igne flammae rubi apparu-
isti, et ei in Sina legem dedisti:
veni ad tedimendum nos in bracchio
extento.

O Adonai and Ruler of the house of
Israel, You appeared to Moses in the
fire of the burning bush, and on Mount
Sinai gave him Your Law. Come,
with an outstretched arm redeem us!

December 19:
(from Isaiah 11:10)

O radix Jesse, qui stas in signum
populorum, super quem continebunt
reges os suum, quem gentes depreca-
buntur: veni ad liberandum nos, iam
noli tardare.

O Root of Jesse, You stand for an ensign
of mankind; before You kings shall keep
silence, and to You all nations shall
have recourse. Come, save us, and do
not delay.

December 20:
(from Isaiah 22:22 and Revelation 3:7)

O clavis David, et sceptrum domus
Israel; qui aperis, et nemo claudit;
claudis, et nemo aperit: veni, et
educ vinctum de domo carceris, se-
dentem in tenebris, et umbra mortis.

O Key of David and Scepter of the house
of Israel: You open and no man closes;
You close and no man opens.
Come, and deliver him from the chains
of prison who sits in darkness and in
the shadows of death.

December 21:
(from Zacharias 6:12)

O Oriens, splendor lucis aeternae, et sol iustitiae: veni, et illumina cedentes in tenebris, et umbra mortis.

O Rising Dawn, Radiance of the Light eternal and Sun of Justice; come, and enlighten those who sit in darkness and in the shadow of death.

December 22:
(from Aggeus 2:8)

O Rex gentium, et desideratus earum, lapisque angularis, qui facis utraque unum: veni, et salva hominem, quem de limo formasti.

O King of the Gentiles, and the Desired of all, You are the cornerstone that binds two into one. Come, and save poor man whom You fashioned out of clay

December 23:
(from Isaiah 7:14 and 8:8)

O Emmanuel, Rex et legifer noster exspectatio gentium, et Salvator earum: veni ad salvandum nos, Domine Deus noster.

O Emmanuel, our King and Lawgiver, the Expected of nations and their Savior: Come, and save us, O Lord our God!

Choir of Monks and Their Leader
late 14th century
French miniature
from La Bible hystoriaux
Bibliothèque Nationale de France, Paris

Glossary

ANTIPHON: a devotional composition sung responsively as part of a liturgy; a short liturgical text chanted responsively before a psalm or canticle

BAROQUE: a style of musical composition that flourished in Europe from 1600 to 1750, marked by chromaticism, strict forms, and elaborate ornamentation

BOOK OF HOURS: an abbreviated prayer book designed for the personal devotions of the laity and arranged according to the canonical hours, or Divine Office

BRASS: wind instruments, such as French horn or trombone, made of brass (an alloy of copper and zinc with other metals of varying amounts)

BREVIARY: an ecclesiastical book consisting of prayers, hymns, and offices for the canonical hours.

CANONICAL HOURS: prescribed times of the day set aside for prayers, or Divine Office; in eight intervals for reciting prayers

CANTATA: a vocal or instrumental composition comprising choruses, solos, and recitation

CANTOR: the chief singer in a synagogue; a person who leads a congregation or choir in singing

CAPPELLA: chapel; a choir traditionally associated with a court or other institution; usually used as a cappella, an abbreviation of "a cappella Sistina," meaning "in the style of the Sistine Chapel," which means unaccompanied polyphonic singing

CARILLON: a set of bells in a tower played from a keyboard or by some other mechanism

CAROL: a song of praise or joy, especially for Christmas; an old round dance often accompanied by singing

CAROLE: French word for dance and principal dance from twelfth to thirteenth centuries in European upper-class circles

CHANT: a song or melody; the body of liturgical plainsong, or music, of the Roman Catholic Church

CHORALE: a Protestant hymn tune; a harmonized hymn, especially one for organ; a chorus or choir

CHORD: a combination of three or more usually concordant tones sounded simultaneously

CHORISTER: a choir singer, usually a choirboy

CHORUS: a musical composition in four or more parts written for a large number of singers; song refrain in which the audience joins the soloist

CLAVICHORD: an early musical keyboard instrument producing soft sounds by tangents striking horizontal strings

CONCERTATO: derived from *concerto* for seventeenth century music involving elements of contrast whereby melody is shared between several different voices in a performance

CONCERTO: a musical work for any combination of voices or instruments

COUNTERPOINT: the combination of two or more independent melodic lines; in general practice a technique of composition called polyphony; since the sixteenth century each line has its own independent rhythmic life

DIVINE OFFICE: the canonical hours or the official rites *(officium)* of the Roman Catholic Church, not including the Mass

ENSEMBLE: a unit or group of complementary parts that contribute to a single effect; two or more vocalists or instrumentalists

FLUTE: a high-pitched musical instrument of the woodwind family that is tubular in shape with finger holes and keys on the side and a reedless mouthpiece

GREGORIAN CHANT: a monophonic liturgical plainsong of the Roman Catholic Church, systemized during the papacy of Gregory I; also called "plainchant"

HARMONY: the simultaneous combination of notes in a chord

HARP: a musical instrument consisting of an upright open triangular frame with forty-six strings of graded lengths that are played by the plucking of fingers

HARPSICHORD: an earlier keyboard instrument in which strings are sounded by means of quill or leather plectrums rather than hammers.

HIGH MASS: a Mass where the Ordinary and the Proper are sung

HORN: a wind instrument generally made of brass

HYMN: a metrical song of praise or thanksgiving to God; any song of praise or joy

KEYBOARD: in music a set of keys, as on a piano or an organ, or in olden times on a harpsichord or virginals

LAUDS: the interval of prayers following Matins and together constitute the first of the canonical hours; formerly the second service of prayers at dawn

LIBRETTO: the text used in an opera or other dramatic musical setting, or a book containing the text; known as "book"

LITURGY: a public act of praise; the worship in the Christian Church

LOW MASS: a Mass recited by the priest without music

LUTE: a stringed instrument shaped like half a pear and with a bent neck with a fretted fingerboard for tuning; a medieval plucking instrument

LYRE: an ancient Greek or Middle Eastern harplike instrument

MACARONIC: pertains to a literary composition containing a mixture of Latin and vernacular words; very prominent in usage during the thirteenth to fifteenth centuries

MADRIGAL: an unaccompanied vocal composition, following a strict poetic form, for two or three voices in simple harmony; became popular form of secular polyphony in late sixteenth century

MASS: the celebration of the Eucharist by Roman Catholics and some Protestant denominations

MATINS: formerly the first of the eight canonical hours; now combined with Lauds to constitute the first of seven canonical hours' morning prayers before sunrise

MINSTREL: medieval musician who traveled from place to place singing and reciting poetry

MINNESINGER: a German medieval minstrel

MONOPHONY: music consisting of a single melodic line

MOTET: a form of sacred music composition for several voices, or polyphony, and usually sung without accompaniment

NEUMES: (plural usage) signs or symbols used in notation and representing the movement of pitch or melody in plainchant, particularly during the medieval period in manuscript transcriptions of Gregorian chant

NOTATION: a system of symbols and notes used to represent a number or value in music, beginning with specially devised letters in Greek music, by neumes in the early medieval age, in tablature for old lute and organ music, and in notes according to our present form; one of the most important developments in the history of music

ORATORIO: a vocal composition, usually for solo voices and chorus with some instrumental accompaniment, or orchestration, telling a sacred story

ORGANUM: musical composition of adding two, three, or more voice parts to a chant melody

ORCHESTRA: a large group of musicians that play together on various instruments, usually including strings, woodwinds, brass, and percussion instruments

PERCUSSION INSTRUMENT: a musical instrument in which sound is produced by striking a resonating surface with a stick, hand, or pedal, such as a drum, castanets, rattle, tambourine, and cymbals

PLAINCHANT: a form of medieval music; plainsong or Gregorian chant

PLAINSONG: Gregorian chant; general designation for various bodies of medieval liturgical music with strict meter and sung without accompaniment

POLYPHONY: simultaneous combination of two or more independent melodic parts, especially when in close harmonic relationship; counterpoint

PSALTER: a book containing some or all musical settings from the book of Psalms

RECITATIVE: a musical style used in opera and oratorio, in which the text is declaimed in the rhythm of natural speech with a slight melodic variation

REFRAIN: a phrase or verse repeated at intervals throughout a song or poem, especially at the end of each stanza

SACKBUT: a medieval musical instrument resembling the trombone; a triangular stringed instrument; also spelled sackbutt

SCHOLA CANTORUM: a specialized group of singers established by the Church after the sixth century and entrusted with ecclesiastical chant formerly sung by the congregation in important churches

SOLO: a musical composition or passage for an individual voice or instrument, with or without accompaniment

SONATA: a musical composition originated in the sixteenth century that is played on instruments as opposed to being sung, evolving in the seventeenth century as compositions for smaller instrumental ensembles and by the nineteenth century mostly used in the composition of large-scale works

STAFF: a set of horizontal lines and their spaces on which musical notes are written (plural: stave)

STRINGS: musical instruments, especially of the violin family, where cords of wires or gut are stretched across the sounding board of an instrument, e.g., harp, guitar, violin, viola, cello, harpsichord, and double bass

SYMPHONY: a lengthy work in sonata form for orchestra, consisting of several movements; harmony, especially of sound or color

TABLATURE: a system of notation that uses numbers, letters, or other signs as an alternate to staff notation, and primarily used for instrumental music for the past 670 years

TROPING: a technique of adding words to an already existing melody or liturgical text

TROUBADOUR: a medieval French minstrel

TROVATORI: a medieval Italian minstrel

TUNE: a simple and easily remembered melody

VESPERS: time of day set aside for prayer, generally a worship service in the late afternoon or evening hours; sixth of the seven canonical hours

VIOLIN: a stringed instrument played with a bow, having four strings tuned at intervals of a fifth, an unfretted fingerboard, and a shallower body than a viol; capable of great flexibility in range, tone, and dynamics; developed quickly during the Baroque period

VIRGINAL(S): a small, legless, rectangular harpsichord popular in the sixteenth and seventeenth centuries; the word is often used in the plural: a pair of virginals

VIRTUOSO: a performer of exceptional skill with particular reference to technical ability; today it has come to mean a performer with artistic skills as well

WIND INSTRUMENT: an instrument in which sound is produced by vibrations of a column of air set in motion by the performer's blowing; two main categories are woodwind (not all made of wood), such as the flute, piccolo, oboe, clarinet, and bassoon, and brass (not all made of brass), such as the horn, trumpet, trombone, and tuba

Bibliography

BOOKS

1 *Baker's Biographical Dictionary of Musicians,* Sixth Edition, Edited by Nicholas Slonimsky. Schirmer Books, New York, 1978.

2 *The Book of Christmas* by Rumer Godden, and *Christmas around the World,* Reader's Digest Association. Pleasantville, New York, 1985.

3 *Christ and the Carols,* William J. Reynolds. Broadman Press, Nashville, 1967.

4 *Christmas Carols: A Reference Guide,* William E. Studwell. Garland Publishing, New York & London, 1985.

5 *Christmas Songs and Their Stories,* Herbert H. Wernecke. The Westminster Press, Philadelphia, 1957.

6 *Collected Hymns & Carols,* John Mason Neale. Hodden & Stroughton, New York, 1914.

7 *Daily Roman Missal,* Edited by the Rev. James Socias. Scepter Publishers & Midwest Theological Forum, Princeton & Chicago, 1993.

8 *Dictionary of Hymnology,* Edited by John Julian. John Murray, London, 1908.

9 *The Encyclopedia of Music,* Edited by Beverly Jollands. Anness Publishing, London, 2002.

10 *Gesantansgabe der musikalischen werke von Michael Praetorius,* Arnold Mendelssohn & Willibald Gurlitt. Edited by Frederick Blume. Wolfenbuttel, Berlin, 1928-1960.

11 *Graduale Romanum,* Abbaye Saint-Pierre De Solesmes. Desclie & Co., Tornai, Belgium, 1974.

12 *Heritage of Music: Volume 1: Classical Music and Its Origins,* Edited by Michael Raeburn and Alan Kendall. Oxford University Press, New York, 1990.

13 *Heritage of Music: Volume 2: The Romantic Era,* Edited by Michael Raeburn and Alan Kendall. Oxford University Press, New York, 1990.

14 *Heritage of Music: Volume 3: The Nineteenth-Century Legacy,* Edited by Michael Raeburn and Alan Kendall. Oxford University Press, New York, 1990.

15 *The History of Civilization: Part III, Caesar and Christ,* Will Durant. Simon and Schuster, New York, 1944.

16 *The History of Civilization: Part IV, The Age of Faith,* Will Durant. Simon and Schuster, New York, 1950.

17 *The History of Civilization: Part V, The Renaissance,* Will Durant. Simon and Schuster, New York, 1953.

18 *The History of Civilization: Part VI, The Reformation,* Will Durant. Simon and Schuster, New York, 1957.

19 *The History of Civilization: Part VII, The Age of Reason Begins,* Will and Ariel Durant. Simon and Schuster, New York, 1961.

20 *The History of Civilization: Part VIII, The Age of Louis XIV,* Will and Ariel Durant. Simon and Schuster, New York, 1963.

21 *The History of Civilization: Part IX, the Age of Voltaire,* Will and Ariel Durant. Simon and Schuster, New York, 1965.

22 *The History of Civilization: Part X, Rosseau and Revolution,* Will and Ariel Durant. Simon and Schuster, New York, 1967.

23 *The Holy Bible Old and New Testaments in the King James Version.* Thomas Nelson Publishers, Nashville-Camden-New York, 1979.

24 *The Hours of the Divine Office in English and Latin.* The Order of St. Benedict, Collegeville, Minnesota, 1963.

25 *How to Read Music: Reading Music Made Simple,* Terry Burrows. Carlton Books, St. Martin's Press, New York, 1999.

26 *The International Book of Christmas Carols,* Walter Ehret & George Evans. Prentice-Hall, Englewood Cliffs, New Jersey, 1963

27 *J.S. Bach Sacred Songs,* Fritz Oberdoerffer. Concordia Publishinghouse, St. Louis, 1958.

28 *Lieber usualis,* Edited by Benedictines of Sloesmes, Society of St. John the Evangelist. Desclie & Co., Tornai, Belgium, 1952.

29 *Liturgin Horarum Iuxta Titum Romanum, Vol. 1: Tempus Adventus & Tempus Nativitatis.* Libreria Editrice, Vatican City, 1965.

30 *The Liturgy for the Hours According to the Roman Rite.* Catholic Book Publishing Co., New York, 1975.

31 *Moravian Youth Hymnal,* The Interprovincial Board of Christian Education. Moravian Choral in America, Bethlehem, PA, 1942.

32 *Music in History: The Evolution of Art,* Third Edition, Howard D. McKinney & W.R. Anderson. American Book Company, New York, 1966.

33 *New Catholic Encyclopedia, Volumes 1-14,* the Most Reverend William J. McDonald, Editor-in-Chief, The Catholic University of America, Washington, DC, 1967.

34 *The New Grove Concise Dictionary of Music,* Edited by Stanley Sadie. Macmillan Press, London, 1988.

35 *The New Grove Dictionary of Music & Musicians, Vols. I-XX,* Edited by Stanley Sadie. Macmillan Publishers, London, 1980.

36 *The New Harvard Dictionary of Music,* Edited by Don Michael Randel. The Belknap Press of Harvard University Press, Boston, 1986.

37 *New Latin-English Sunday Missal.* Association for the Latin Liturgy, Vatican Press, 1987. English translations from International Commission on the Liturgy.

38 *Noëls: A New Collection of Old Carols,* Max and Anne Oberndorfer. H.T. FitzSimons, Chicago, 1932.

39 *The Oxford Book of Carols,* Percy Dearmer, Ralph Vaughan Williams, and Martin Shaw. Oxford University Press, London, 1928.

40 *Polyhymnia caduceatris et panegyrica, Vol. 17, No. XI,* Michael Praetorius, 1619. See *Gesantansgabe der musikalischenwerke von Michael Praetorius.*

41 *Publishing Glad Tidings: Essays on Christmas Music,* William E. Studwell and Dorothy E. Jones. The Haworth Press, New York & London, 1998.

42 *Saint Joseph Daily Missal,* Edited by Rev. Hugo H. Hoever, S.O. Cist., PhD, Catholic Book Publishing, New York, 1957.

43 *Saints for All Seasons,* Victor J. Green. Avenel Books, New York, 1982.

44 *The St. Gregory Hymnal and Catholic Choir Book,* Edited and arranged by Nicola A. Montani. The St. Gregory Guild, Philadelphia, 1920.

45 *Silent Night, Holy Night: The Immortal Song and Its Origin,* Michael Gundringer. Lamprechtshausen, Salzburg, c.1950.

46 *Silent Night, Holy Night: The Story of a Lovely Christmas Song.* The Frederick H. Jaenicken Company, Chicago, 1935.

47 *Stories Behind the Best-Loved Songs of Christmas,* Ace Collins. Zondervan, Grand Rapids, MI, 2001.

48 *The Summit Choir Book,* The Dominican Nuns of Summit, New Jersey. Monastery of Our Lady of the Rosary, 1983.

49 *Texts of the Choral Works of Johann Sebastian Bach in English Translations,* Vol. 12, Henry S. Drinker. Association of American Colleges Arts Program, New York, 1942-43.

50 *Tidings True, Medieval Carols, Vol.4 of Musica Britannia,* Edited by John Stevens. Stainer & Bell, London, 1952.

51 *Today's Missal: Advent/Ordinary Time,* Edited by Bari Colomari. Oregon Press, Portland, 1994.

52 *Translations and Annotations of Choral Repertoire, Sacred Latin Texts,* Edited & annotated by Ron Jeffers. Earthsongs, Corvallis, Oregon, 1988.

OTHER SOURCES

1 *Bring a Torch, A Christmas Celebration,* The Kenneth Jewell Chorale. Detroit, The Musical Heritage Society/MHS Stereo 3667; notes by Dalos Grobe.

2 *The Canonical Hours,* Catholic Webrings, (kensmen.com/catholic/hours.html).

3 *A Child Is Born,* The Trappist Monks of the Abbey of Our Lady of Gethsemani. Columbia Records, ML 5310, released as CD A26303, 1995.

4 *Christmas Music from Medieval and Renaissance Europe,* The Sixteen Harry Christophers. The Musical Heritage Society/514251H, 1987; notes by Nicholas Robertson.

5 *Encarta Multimedia Encyclopedia.* Microsoft Corp., CD-ROM, 1993.

6 *Gregorian Chant: Chants for Christmastide,* Scola of the Hofburgkapelle. Vienna, The Musical Heritage Society, 1989.

7 *History of the Organ,* The Copernicus Education Gateway. EdGate.com, Inc., 2000, (panther.bsc.edu).

8 *A History of the Hymns and Carols of Christmas,* Douglas D. Anderson, (hymnsandcarolsofchristmas.com).

9 *Hört zu ihr lieben Leute,* George Kallmeyer Verlag, Wolfenbuttel-Berlin, 1928.

10 *The Hutchinson Encyclopedia of Music.* Helicon Publishing, CD-ROM, 1996.

11 Information provided by Prof. Scott Foglesong, Chair, Music Theory and Musicianship, San Francisco Music Conservatory, CA, December 29, 2002.

12 Information provided by Prof. John Poole, Choral Conducting, School of Music at the University of Indiana, Bloomington, IN, February 26, 2003.

13 *Jesu, Joy of Man's Desiring,* Oxford University Press, London, 1926.

14 Latin-English text provided by Prof. Gerald Malsbary of St. Charles Seminary, Wynnewood, PA, January 15, 1994.

15 *Liturgies: Western Catholic Liturgies* (liturgica.com), Benjamin D. Williams, 2007.

16 *The Lord's Prayer,* John Charles Thomas, Album of Favorite Songs & Arias, G. Schirmer, Inc. New York, 1946.

17 *The Lord's Prayer, Vol. II,* The Mormon Tabernacle Choir, Alexander Schreiner & Frank Asper, organ & The Philadelphia Orchestra. Columbia Stereo Records MS 6367; notes by Jay Welch.

18 *Mass,* Encyclopædia Orbis Latini, © Zdravko Batzarov (orbilat.com).

19 Medieval Writing: History, Heritage and Data Source, Dr. John Tillotson, Australian National University in Canberra, Australia, and Dr. Dianne Tillotson, multimedia Web author, 2001 (medievalwriting.50megs.com).

20 *Messiah,* The Philadelphia Orchestra and Mormon Tabernacle Choir. Columbia Records Master-works/M2L263; notes by Jay Welch.

21 *Messiah and George Frederic Handel,* Issue #147. Christian History Institute (gospelcom.net).

22 *The Messiah: An Oratorio,* G.F. Handel; *G. Schirmer Editions of Oratorios and Cantatas;* G. Schirmer, Inc., New York/London, 1912

23 *Michael Praetorius, Canticum Trium Puerorum, FIVE MOTETS,* Audite Chorale of Paris,

Recorder Ensemble of Paris, "Les Saqueboutiers" Instrumental Ensemble. The Musical Heritage Society/MHS 7434Y, 1986; notes by Marc Vignal & translated by John Underwood.

24 *Music History 102: The Middle Ages.* The Internet Public Library (ipl.org).

25 *Music of Tudor and Jacobean England,* Peter Watchorn, harpsichord. Musica Omnia, Missouri, 1996; notes by Howard Schott.

26 *New Advent: The Catholic Encyclopedia,* Volumes I-XV, Copyright © 1907-1912 by Robert Appleton Company. Online Edition Copyright © 2003 by Kevin Knight (newadvent.org).

27 *O Magnum Mysterium,* Thomas Ludovice Victoria: Abulensis Motets & Masses, Vol.1, Breitkopf & Hartel, Wiesbaden, 1902.

28 *Panis angelicus,* G. Schirmer, Inc. New York, 1908.

29 *The Penguin Dictionary of Music,* Arthur Jacobs, 1997 (www.xfer.com).

30 *The Vienna Choir Boys Christmas Festival,* Vienna Choir Boys. RCA Records/PRLl220, 1976.

$\mathcal{N}$otes

The corresponding Numbers to this Notes section are found in the Bibliography.
A numbers for Book Titles
B numbers for Other Sources

The Historical Perspective

A04, pp. 379–381
A10, pp. 26–29, 254–255
A13, pp. 28-38
A16, pp. 749–750
A17, pp. 896–900
A18, pp. 603–604
A19, pp. 778–782
A20, pp. 253, 546
A21, p. 266
A22, pp. 224, 407
A23, p. 527
A32, pp. 294–306
A34, Vol. 3, p. 450
    Vol. 10, pp.105-125
    Vol. 14, p.315
A39
B5, 7, 8, 11, 12, 15, 12, 24,
    27, 29

Music Collection

1 Anima nostra A23, 28, 33, 35; B30
2 Concerto Grosso in G Minor, Op. 6/8 A9, 32, 35;
    B4, 5, 10, 29
3 Gloria A9, 12, 34, 36; B10
4 Gregorian Chant A7, 9, 11, 12, 23, 24, 25, 29,
    30, 33, 37, 42, 44, 51, 52; B2, 3, 6, 8, 18,
    25, 26
5 Hodie Christus natus est A23, 28, 35, 38, 52 ; B5
6 Hört zu ihr lieben Leute A10, 35, 40; B9, 23
7 Jesu, bleibet mein freude A4, 9, 23, 26, 35, 50;
    B10, 13
8 Kyrie A9, 12, 18, 34, 35, 36; B10, 26
9 The Lord's Prayer A1, 23, 42, 52; B16, 17, 26
10 Messiah A9, 13, 23; B20, 21, 22
11 O magnum mysterium A9, 28, 35, 52; B1, 27
12 Panis angelicus A9, 14, 49; B8, 14, 28
13 Stille nacht, heilige nacht A4, 5, 26, 35, 45,
    46; B8
14 Veni, Emmanuel A3, 5, 24, 26, 31, 34, 41, 47,
    48, 52; B8

Title Index

Audio Index

Title	Performed By
Hört zu ihr lieben Leute	Viva Voce Ensemble ℗1999, BIS Records AB, Åkersberga. With kind permission from BIS Records—www.bis.se. Copyright BIS Records AB 1999.
O Come, O Come Emmanuel (*Veni, Emmanuel*)	Leslie Pearson and John Paice, with The London Bell Ringers Courtesy of Reader's Digest Music
Jesu, Joy of Man's Desiring (*Jesu, bleibet mein freude*)	The Mormon Tabernacle Choir with the Columbia Symphony Orchestra; Jerold D. Ottley, conductor ℗1981 SONY BMG MUSIC ENTERTAINMENT
Concerto Grosso in G Minor, Op.6/8 (Christmas Concerto) *I. Vivace-Grave. Arcate, sostenuto e come sta, II. Allegro, III. Adagio-Allegro-Adagio, IV. Vivace, V. Allegro, VI. Largo. Pastorale ad libitum*	Kammerorchester Carl Philipp Emanuel Bach; Hartmut Haenchen, conductor; Raphael Alperman, harpsichord; Thorsten Rosenbusch and Christian. Trompler, violin; Harald Winkler, bass; Karl-Heinz Schröter, cello ℗1993 Sony Classical, a division of Sony Entertainment Holdings GmbH
O Magnum Mysterium	Westminster Cathedral Choir; David Hill, conductor ℗Hyperion Records Ltd, London, 1986 Courtesy of Hyperion Records Ltd, London 1986 www.hyperion-records.co.uk
Kyrie	Gabrieli Players with the Gabrieli Consort; Paul McCreesh, conductor ℗1993 Deutsche Grammophon GmbH, Hamburg, Courtesy of Deutsche Grammophon GmbH, Hamburg under license from Universal Music Enterprises
Gloria	Harvard Glee Club ℗1996 Harvard Glee Club Courtesy of The Harvard Glee Club

Title	Performed By
Gradual: *Tecum Principium*	The Trappist Monks of the Abbey of Gethsemani. Originally Released 1958. All rights reserved by SONY BMG MUSIC ENTERTAINMENT
Messiah: For Unto Us a Child Is Born	English Baroque Soloists with the Monteverdi Choir; John Eliot Gardiner, conductor 1983 Universal International Music B.V. Courtesy of Polydor Ltd. (UK) under license from Universal Music Enterprises
Alleluia: *Dominus Dixit*	The Trappist Monks of the Abbey of Gethsemani. Originally Released 1958. All rights reserved by SONY BMG MUSIC ENTERTAINMENT
Anima Nostra	The Vienna Boys Choir; Hans Gillesberger, conductor ℗1976 BMG Ariola Hamburg GmbH
Panis Angelicus	Placido Domingo with the Vienna Boys Choir ℗ 1979 BMG Ariola Hamburg GmbH
Messiah: Hallelujah Chorus	English Baroque Soloists with the Monteverdi Choir; John Eliot Gardiner, conductor ℗1983 Universal International Music B.V. Courtesy of Polydor Ltd. (UK) under license from Universal Music Enterprises
The Lord's Prayer	The Mormon Tabernacle Choir with the Philadelphia Orchestra; Eugene Ormandy, conductor. Originally Recorded 1962. All rights reserved by SONY BMG MUSIC ENTERTAINMENT
Hodie Christus Natus Est	The Cathedral Choir of St. John the Divine, Richard Westenburg, conductor ℗1993 Vanguard Classics Courtesy of Vanguard Classics/Sheridan Square Entertainment
Silent Night *(Stille nacht, heilige nacht)*	John Klein, carillon Originally Recorded 1957. All rights reserved by SONY BMG MUSIC ENTERTAINMENT